With the clock ticking down in the fourth period, the score stood at 24-22 with Calais leading. They missed a shot with only seven seconds left in the game, and the stands went suddenly silent when the ball ended up in Tiffany's hands. She raced to the middle of the court, leapt high above her Calais defenders, and fired the ball towards the net. A split second after it left her hands, the buzzer sounded and she collapsed to the floor.

All eyes watched the ball soar above the court, a high arching trajectory, moving in slow-motion towards destiny and taking forever to get there. When it passed through the hoop, hardly ruffling the net, the crowd erupted. I don't know how many noted, at least at first, that Tiffany lay in a heap mid-court, sobbing, surrounded by her team-mates. Buster was one of the first to her side, ahead of the coach. She may not have even seen her scoring shot.

We gathered up our things and headed towards the door. Most times the end of a game would be a noisy event with neighbors greeting each other and friendly banter passing freely, but not so this time. Many had tears trickling down and some cried openly. Few spoke and when they did it was in muted tones. Even the Calais boosters recognized that something special had just happened and respected the moment.

Buster Loman

A Down East Story
by
JD Rule

December, 2017

JD Rule
PO Box 519
Lubec, ME 04652

© JD Rule 2017

jdrule@lubecscribbler.com
www.lubecscribbler.com

Published by South Bay Associates
December, 2017

ISBN-13: 978-1979690393

Other works by JD Rule

<u>The Delsey Trilogy</u>

Bridge to Someday
Delsey
Johnson Canyon

<u>Down East Stories</u>

Neap Tide
Monument Lot
Cold Harbor

Voices
Orion's Belt & Alnilam
Murphy's Revisited
Mowry Beach

Buster Loman

Contents

Dedicated to all who struggle.

Rogue Wave

<u>All Fun and Games</u>

"Don't know 'bout this stuff, Arnie." Jake, a tall angular man all elbows, sat at the bar in Annie's Place with the yellow suspenders of his bib waterproofs draped across his lap. The big-city newspaper lay in front of him, open to a list of the president-elect's cabinet picks. "I jist don't know about all this." He looked like he was about to cry.

"But you voted for him," I reminded him, just in case he forgot. "At least you told me you were going to."

"I know I did. So'd most of my fam'ly. But *this* ain't what we was looking for."

"What'd you *think* the result would be?"

"We jist wanted shake things up a bit." Jake glowered into the bottom of his glass like more beer would appear if he would just look hard enough. "Kind of like a shot across the bow, you get my drift. Remind 'em we're out here."

Beyond the bar's back door, out over the deck, Canada loomed just across the narrows from a border town that was so far to the east that most Americans didn't even know we existed. A spitting snow squall didn't quite obscure the view across the water and the small lighthouse cast a glimmering path across the current.

Here in Flagg's Point we'd been hearing jokes for a long time how those people over there on the other side of the channel were going to build a wall to keep Americans out should he win, but just a few weeks ago that gag lost its punchline, one day to the next. We woke up on the ninth of November nervously wondering what the future would bring, hoping for the best but fearing the worst. By now, three weeks later, the gnawing uncertainty had begun to sink in.

Couldn't call the feeling 'numbing' because it didn't lessen with time, maybe a better word was 'scary'.

"So," I replied, "instead we're gonna sink the whole damn ship."

"Never 'spected the guy *could* win or even that he *wanted* to. All them friggin' polls sed he was dead meat, we jist figgered we was sending a message."

"So he fooled enough of us, now he's the one."

"Guess so." He grimaced and looked again into the bottom of his glass. "Guy don't have a friggin' *clue* what he's doing." He waved his hand dismissively at the paper. "Look at all them jerks he's dragging in with him. Each one's worse than the last."

"Hey," I said, waving Annie over to serve up another round. "Give the guy a break. Larry, Curly, and what was his name? Moe! Only names in his phonebook so now his new Chief of Staff gets to pay off his *own* debts. You said you wanted a 'bloody outsider'." Jake looked at me funny. "I remember you said that."

"Go 'head, rub it in, would'ja? I know I did." He looked down with a grimace, muttering. "Looks like *'bloody'* gonna be the right word." He fell silent, turning to watch the two girls at the pool table. Keisha, a tall slender black girl, maybe early twenties, continued to score points against a solidly built blonde with hoop earrings, about the same age but three inches shorter. Blondie watched in dismay as Keisha dropped a string of balls, each properly called, with no wasted motions. The two of them paid us no nevermind, just a couple of old guys crying in their beer.

The mugs were delivered and Jake turned back to the bar. "Thanks," he said, lifting the glass. "What kind of a world we gonna create for the likes o' them?" He gestured with his thumb at the two girls, both of whom continued to ignore us.

"What kind of a world *we* gonna have," I asked him. "Just because we're old farts don't mean we don't count."

"Yeah, yeah, yeah," he grumbled. "We both got grandkids. Don't you worry 'bout them?"

"Course I do. They're the ones gonna *pay* for this. Big time. I'm afraid for how he might screw up our environment."

"That victory speech o' his ..." Jake slumped down like he was giving up. "Said he'd 'renew the American Dream'. Didn't say nothing 'bout *shredding* it."

A sudden gust of wind whistled through the front door, momentarily darkened by the broad-shouldered bulk of Buster Loman. A few errant snowflakes followed him in. A glance out the door showed a good flurry underway but nothing likely to last.

Buster wore the same bright yellow waterproofs as Jake but also sported a red baseball cap with a few illegible words showing through the dirt. The visible part said something like "Make America..." but the rest was obscured. He shook off the cold and plopped down wearily on the seat next to Jake. Casually reaching over, Jake knocked a few bits of ice off the back of Buster's jacket.

"What'd you get for them scallops?" Buster gestured for a beer and turned towards Jake.

"'Leven bucks. You?"

"The same. Took me seven pulls hit the quota. You?"

"Five."

"Wish I knew *your* tricks," grumbled Buster.

Jake glanced up at Buster's hat. "How long you gonna wear that thing?" I felt his elbow giving me a sneaky poke in the ribs.

"Bothers you, don't it."

"*Bothers* me?" Jake laughed softly and took a swig of beer. "Think it's stupid."

"Hey brother!" Buster whirled around on the stool and glanced over at me. "America's gonna be *great* again." He poked his finger at Jake. "You was at that Bangor rally too."

"I was," admitted Jake. "Way he talked he had me convinced, just like you."

Buster grabbed his beer and turned towards me. "All them fine speeches, way he got the crowd all riled up, it's gonna be *great*!" He took a gulp and wiped his mouth with the back of his hand. "Don'cha think so, Arnie?"

The loud 'crack' from the pool table interrupted us. Keisha had just broken again and Blondie stood aside with a glum look. I turned back towards Buster. "Not sure we ever *stopped* being great."

Jake guffawed loudly and looked straight at Buster. "Mebbe that's what done happened Election Day."

"What's this?" Buster sat back, his eyes shifting back and forth between the two of us. "You guys ganging up on me?"

"C'mon Buster," said Jake, laughing even louder. "How long've we known each other? Hell, time was, I even let you date my sister."

"What do you mean, you 'let me'?"

"You saying it ain't so?"

"Well…" Buster glanced at me again like he was hoping for cover. My deadpan expression must have unsettled him. "I got it. You voted for her." He glanced again at me. "Prolly *both* of you."

"Don't know about Arnie," said Jake. "I voted for the one I thought knew what he was doing, a'fore I come to know he *don't.*"

Buster shot Jake a defiant stare. "Can't you give the guy a chance?"

"Kind'a late now," Jake admitted. "Don't have much choice." I didn't say anything, just laughed.

"That's not how you was talking *before* the election." Buster turned away from the two of us. I didn't really think he was interested in the boat heading up the channel with a flock of noisy birds in hot pursuit.

"Yeah, I know," replied Jake. "Back then it was all fun and games. Play acting."

"That's how you saw it?"

"You din't?"

"Arnie…" Buster shot me an angry look. "You ain't saying nothing."

"Me?" I stifled a laugh. "Never said I was voting for him."

"You're gonna put this in one of them stupid novels you write, ain't you." When I didn't respond, he continued. "Anyway, you never tole us who it was you *was* voting for."

"Was I *s'posed* to?" Buster turned away with a growl; Jake chuckled like he'd been caught in a lie. I sensed someone standing behind me – it was Keisha. Apparently she had finally missed a shot because Blondie was lining up on the two-ball. She caught my glance and snickered, picked up her beer and returned to the table, probably expecting it'd be her turn again soon.

"So why you thinking different now?" Buster apparently felt that Jake had abandoned him, the way he closed in on him.

"Buster, you member when we was kids…" Jake took another swig of beer and turned his way. "When we'd play pick-up basketball?"

"What's basketball got to do with anything?"

A wistful smile crossed his craggy face. "Member what happened when all the best players landed on the *other* team?" He paused and laughed like he was recalling one particular game from long ago. "You got your clock cleaned."

"You saying he ain't getting good people?"

Jake glanced down at the newspaper. "Not saying nothing."

The conversation fell into silence for a few minutes. I ordered myself another beer and waited. A cheer from the table announced the end of the game. Keisha drifted over to the bar, followed by Blondie. They sat down nearby and Buster eyed both.

"Keisha," said Jake. "What do *you* think of all this?"

"What," she replied with a bit of a nervous giggle, "do I think of *what*?"

"I know you better'n that," he replied. "You don't want to say nothing."

"What would you expect me to say?" She wasn't giggling any more. "I read the papers too."

"If you was a woman," interjected Blondie, leveling a hard stare at Jake. "What would *you* be saying?"

Buster turned away with a loud harrumph and Jake stared at her slack-jawed. "I din't go to that rally," she continued, "and for sure they wouldn't let Keisha in if she *did* go." She drained her beer and signaled for another. "If she *did* get in," she added, "there were jerks there'd throw her out – or worse." Blondie was looking at Buster when she said that but he was looking away. I spotted his white knuckles and the way his breath came in gulps.

"Do *you* know where this thing's going?" asked Keisha, looking towards Jake.

"I'm telling you, he's gonna make America *great* again," replied Buster, now speaking loudly. "Unless," he added, jabbing a finger in her face, "people like *you* don't let him." By this time his face was almost the color of his hat.

"If he could actually *do* that," she countered, "could someone like *me* really stop him?"

"Maybe," said Jake, "he could start by telling us what he means."

"You was at that rally," said Buster. "I seen you there."

"Already said I was there," Jake confirmed. "I done heard ever word he said." He turned back to the bar. "Haven't seen anything since then says he knows how to steer that boat home."

"Can't you just trust him?"

"Buster," replied Jake. "Long's I've knowed you, and it's been a long time, never knowed *you* to trust *no* politician, din't matter what party."

"This time," snarled Buster, "things're diff'runt. He's the one gonna get it done."

"Hah!" called out Keisha. "Compared to what they've done to *my* kind, they've already been good to *his* kind."

Buster glowered across the bar. "Figger'd *you* to play that card," he muttered.

"You think he speaks for *you*?" asked Blondie. "Really?" The scarlet tinge to her ears was only partially concealed by her blonde hair.

"Let me guess," added Keisha. "He's going to reopen the sardine plants."

"First he'll have to close down a bunch of 'em in Thailand and Norway," I ventured. "And the ruins of the last one here are half collapsed and ready to go."

"Good thing if that heap goes 'way," said Jake. "Place is dangerous."

"Maybe he'll bring back the cod," laughed Blondie. "That'd make my grandfather happy."

"I don't get you guys," grumbled Buster. "Don't you want them jobs come back?"

"Those jobs?" Blondie turned to Jake. "You started out fishing with my father thirty years back. You tell us, what would it take for the canneries t'come back?"

"Well, for starters," drawled Jake, "the herring fishery'll have to come back first. They can't *can* 'em if we can't *catch* 'em."

Buster tossed down a five for another beer and turned back towards me. "Sounds like you're saying they ain't nothing we can do."

"How 'bout we use what we got?"

Buster whirled to face me straight on. "The hell you talking 'bout?"

"Every summer," I said, "we get maybe three, four thousand people come through here. What're *they* looking for?"

"Damn if I know," muttered Buster. "We're a fishing village, not a friggin' tourist trap."

"So," I asked, "the jobs the tourists bring, they're the wrong *kind* of jobs. Is that it?"

"Them ain't *real* jobs." Buster clenched his arms across his chest and glowered. "Jake and me, we're the ones here got *real* jobs."

"So," said Keisha, "the paycheck I get isn't real? And hers too?"

"You can't wait tables all year. Them places all close after Labor Day."

"And you can't drag scallops all year," interjected Blondie. "Off season *you* do what we *all* do. Find other things need getting done."

"Time was…" Buster waved his right hand towards the waterfront alongside the channel. "There was nothing here *but* boats. Solid line of 'em, worked all year 'round."

"And when was that?" asked Jake. "Maybe 1916? You know it ain't been *that* way since 'bout then."

"Your guy wants to take the country *back* a hundred years?" Blondie laughed out loud. "Lemme off that boat, okay?"

"Go ahead and deny it, we was great back then," growled Buster.

Keisha put her beer down and scowled at Buster. "Not according to what my great-grandma used to say. Those times back then… They were not so great."

"Women couldn't even vote that year," added Blondie. "That's what he wants to do?"

Buster was adamant. "When do you guys think we *was* great?"

"How 'bout right now," I said. "I think we're doing pretty well. From what your guy lets us believe, *he's* done quite well for himself."

Buster's lips quivered behind his beard and his eyes narrowed to slits. "Sounds like you don't want us to be great."

"That's not it," I replied. "Tell me, how often can you believe *any* politician? Specially one who keeps things secret others make public."

He slammed his beer down on the counter and whirled towards the open floor. "You guys c'n mess with *me* all you want," he shouted out. "Jist you 'member, we're the ones what *won* and now he's gonna do things the way *we* want him to." The front door slammed and Buster Loman disappeared into a swirl of snow, almost knocking Adam Russell off his feet.

* * * * *

I should explain that, except to the people who live here, Flagg's Point is probably not the most important town in the nation's easternmost county, although its twelve hundred or so residents qualify it as one of the larger. Our friends asked, and continue to ask, why Evelyn and I moved way out here to Downeast Maine when they were all heading to more benign climes. Sometimes in the depth of the winter when the restaurants are shuttered and the snow piles higher than the porch railing, so do I. But then I get out among the people and the question fades away. When spring finally breaks free the question is set aside until the next winter. The Neptune's Bride big deal in April, when people dress up like they're getting hitched and march down the slushy street to the boat ramp, making as much of a ruckus as they can, that event marks the end of winter. Enough booze floats around that day they keep the kids locked up.

The question never comes up when scallops are on the menu, and those times I've hitched a ride on a boat and eaten them right off the shell I know why fishermen shrug off the risks inherent in their trade. So I go back to my writing, either for the local paper or whatever novel I'm working on, but now with a renewed point of view.

Of course, on the shores of Cobscook Bay, the size of the community is all relative. Clinging to the end of a peninsula surrounded by salt water with twenty-foot tides, devoid of natural resources beyond those meted out by a jealous Neptune, it lies in the heart of a region once the locus of conflicting claims held by competing French and British colonial aspirations, and four centuries later both languages are still heard.

11

No one knows for sure how populous the native settlements were prior to the 1604 arrival of the Europeans, but the Passamaquoddy Tribe continues to live in harmony with, and draw sustenance from, the turbulent waters. Pierre Dugua, Sieur de Mons, and friends occupied what is now called St. Croix Island for only one miserable winter, but that was the start of it all. They called it *L'Acadie*, presaging what was to come. Early images, including some from French explorers, depict Native Americans preserving herring taken from Cobscook waters – chiefly through the use of weirs. Europeans quickly caught on, then introduced more efficient harvesting methods that ultimately started many important fisheries down the slope towards depletion, despite howls of protest from horrified Passamaquoddy fishermen.

Living on the water has been a way of life here for hundreds or maybe thousands of years, particularly given the lack of alternatives. The railroad never reached out to Flagg's Point, and only in the last century did the roads become passable year round. To a young person in the eighteenth and nineteenth centuries living – and often dying – under sail was just the way it was.

Sail has fallen way to the marvelous engine of Rudolf Diesel, but the water beneath the keel remains deep, cold, and unforgiving. This familiarity, coupled with a profound understanding of the local currents, also opened up another lucrative form of employment: smuggling. Eagle-eyed customs officers on both sides of the border discourage modern-day folks from straying too far from the law, but many young people still define themselves in the same manner as their forebears: by their relationship with the sea.

The line between British New Brunswick and Maine was not settled until 1842 when President John Tyler inked the Webster-Ashburton Treaty, a quarter-century before Canada came into being, prompted largely by the American Civil War. Even today there are disputed lines and lands, but many local families predate both of those events, as seen in the matching surnames on both sides. Only in very recent years has the official insistence on passports put a crimp on cross-border picnics and romances.

Towards the end of the nineteenth century the business of preserving fish graduated from the traditional smoking, salting, and pickling into more commercial methods. For four generations the region was the Sardine Capital of the World. Those who did not labor on the sea, labored because of the sea.

These days many see the coveted lobsterman's license as the best way to prosperity, but it is not easily got. The 'student path' was designed so families could pass the business down but eligibility requires that years of work be completed before the eighteenth birthday. For most, the 'apprentice path' is the only option – it requires the same work to be completed, but then the applicant goes on a list waiting for others to retire their licenses. Some languish a lifetime on that list, rising to the top decades later.

For those with licenses, their livelihood is still jeopardized by market, fuel, and bait prices, the lurking threat of environmental and regulatory challenges, and the hazards of the sea. At least regulatory changes that alter the economics of the 'limited entry' fishery can be addressed through political activism. It is often said that the only time fishermen agree on anything is when one of their number is to be hanged.

In modern times outsiders have discovered other charms: elements of nature often taken for granted by those whose families are rooted here. Ocean surf crashing against rocky cliffs, sea-smoke blowing across the bay like a burst feather-pillow, moss-shrouded trails snaking through luxuriant woods, and the abundance of seafood have attracted visitors seeking the clichéd visions lovingly described in tourist brochures, and some decide to stay on. Most of the time, they share a comfortable relationship with the locals. My relationship is sometimes rocky, however I do try to not give unnecessary offense.

But I digress.

* * * * *

It had been a dreary winter, and the dismal parade of news from Washington didn't make it any better. The weeks seemed to drag by, and all the while the sky remained a pool of lead looming overhead threatening to drop on us with a 'thud.' The temperature wasn't the problem, or maybe it was. In Downeast Maine, January and February are expected to be stormy, but not with the massive snowdrifts the news reports gleefully describe from inland points farther north. Here, the ocean tempers the tempest, but the wind and ice make up for it. By the time spring led us to the mud season, the mood of the town progressed from ugly through grumpy, to merely guardedly pessimistic. Divisions persisted, but those are simply a fact of life. We all awaited the emergence of the crocuses, the reopening of the restaurants, the start of the lobster season, and the return of the blackflies. The things that made up life as we knew it.

I tried to bury myself in the Civil War novel I'd been writing for three years, but it was tough concentrating. Evelyn kept herself busy with her painting, preparing for the upcoming season in Flagg's Point and also a series of juried shows across the country she'd been accepted into and looked forward to attending and sometimes speaking at. We shared a home and a bed, but often moved in different worlds. I envied my wife's ability to tune out distractions.

Events in Washington seemed so far away, yet at the same time so up close and personal. Every day there was something new and absurdly inexplicable, and each was so removed from what had always been considered 'normal' that we wondered what that word actually meant.

So far none of it had directly affected life in Flagg's Point, at least so far as was obvious, but each of us had our own set of expectations. Some of us hailed the new president's cabinet appointees as the saviors that would make life again worth living but others decried them as threats to the way life was supposed to be. From what we were reading, the divisions in Flagg's Point were no different than those seen elsewhere. I for one had grown weary of guarding each of my words lest they start the war all over again.

The change was subtle, although the incidents marking its passage were anything but. Jake maybe said it better than anyone. "I've known some o'them guys all my life," he confided over a beer. "Any more, they'd sooner bite off your head than talk things out, specially if it means admitting maybe you was right 'bout something they seen different."

"Have they changed?" I asked.

"Maybe," he mumbled. "They still be good people and I'd work their boat if they ast me, but *something* has changed. Since when…" He turned to look out over the channel. "Has 'compromise' been a cuss word?"

He finished his beer and we both headed out into the dusk.

We started hearing about sea water temperatures in May being what was expected in July, and the lobstermen geared up early. Stacks of traps appeared alongside the town ramp, then vanished again as they migrated from dooryards to boats to the sea. I didn't see Jake around as often as before, but often spotted his boat, *Three Nines Fine*, heading out the channel laden with traps and blue plastic barrels full of bait, trailing a swarm of birds. At least some things continued like normal.

<u>Twist and Shout</u>

I hadn't seen her before, but it was her long, slender fingers that gave her away, even before I spotted the huge ring. Clearly, this was not a woman used to the kind of work many women do in Flagg's Point.

She sat lounging at the bar, holding a glass of wine, looking about at the big mural and the other decorations. Maybe fifty, carefully dressed, she looked intelligent and approachable. She also looked to be alone, despite that ring. When I sat down nearby she turned my way and smiled.

Reaching for the beer Annie knew I was going to order, I turned back towards her. "You're a visitor. Welcome to Flagg's Point."

It was always easy to strike up a conversation in Annie's place; it had the atmosphere of someone's casual kitchen where nobody was a stranger, and to spot visitors in early June was no big deal. Besides, in a town small as Flagg's Point, if a guy got fresh his wife would know of it before he got home.

She turned my way with one eyebrow lifted. "Am I that obvious?"

"Maybe a little presumptuous of me, I guess." After exchanging the usual pleasantries she told me she was here from Pennsylvania, staying in town for the summer. By trade a graphic designer, and by avocation, as she put it, "a collector of images."

"Call me Lisa," she said.

"And I'm Arnie," I replied. "So what has lured Lisa from Pennsylvania all the way out to the beginning of the known world?"

"Someplace different," she shrugged, turning to look out across the channel, where the Canadian flag fluttered above the customs station, just at the end of the bridge linking two nations. "So are you going to tell me about your town?"

"What would you like to know?"

"For starters, why are there so many empty storefronts?"

I've spoken to many visitors, but this was the first time I'd been hit point blank by *that* question. "These days," I ventured, "if you can't make enough in the summer to keep you going all year..."

"These days? So it hasn't always this way."

"No," I replied sadly, "it has not been."

"How do they do it here?" She gestured around the bar. Compared to places farther south, it did have a bit of a provincial appearance. Painted plywood floor with scuff marks left by dancers with rugged shoes, open ceiling darkened by past years of smoke, decorated with the detritus of a rough and tumble life on the edge. The deck out back lured locals and visitors alike when the weather was warm. At this point, other than Annie, we were the only ones there.

"Even in February, people need a place to rub elbows, get a drink." Frankly, I never understood how Annie did it. I suspected that during the lean months she paid more for heat than she could dream of making across the bar, and probably kept the place open so she'd have someone to talk to.

Lisa was apparently not going to take the short answer. "You said 'these days.' So the town hasn't always been like this."

"No, it hasn't." I didn't know how much she wanted, or how much I wanted to give. 'But,' I said to myself, 'what the hell. Let's see how much this lady wants.'

"Town's reinvented itself twice already," I said. "Some of us're hoping for a third."

Lisa flagged Annie down for a refill and sat back. Her expression said she was hoping I'd say more but was reluctant to ask.

"First it was shipbuilding," I said, watching for her reaction, "then sardine packing."

"The sardine part I've seen," she replied, sipping her wine. "That's pretty well told over at the Historical Society museum." She paused like she was taking mental notes. "What's this about shipbuilding?"

"You go into the forest," I said, "you won't find many oaks. Pretty much they all went to sea."

"Go on."

"Back before the Civil War, it was the biggest thing here. Big square riggers, even a few Clippers. Built in yards up and down these shores. That ended with the shift to iron ships driven by steam engines. No advantage to doing *them* here."

"So then it was sardines?"

"They were smoking fish long before Europeans got here, only way to preserve them. The Franco-Prussian war gave it the boost. Created a demand in New York City for pickled herring, investors figured out they could get them here and make a buck. Time was, Flagg's Point was the Sardine Capital of the World."

"So what killed it?"

"Hah!" I called for another beer. "You trying to get me killed?"

"What?"

"You ask five people that question, around here you'll get six answers. Maybe seven."

"What," she asked, looking across her glass, "do *you* say?"

"I actually studied that once. Went to the State Archives to see what was there."

"And you found?"

"During World War II they sold almost the entire pack to the Army. When the war ended, Morocco wanted in and the local companies had let the business part of it go. Had no marketing or distribution, so they lost out. It's all in the records. To make it worse, since modern refrigeration had already taken over, there was no more need to preserve food so tins of sardines became a luxury instead of a commodity. The industry went upscale, and our guys let it go."

"How about fishing?"

"Yeah," I said, watching as Adam Russell's red and green boat rumbled up the channel with his two crewmen lounging near the stern, apparently enjoying the warm sun. The *Mary Lynne* was rigged for lobstering and from the growl echoing across the water appeared to be heavily laden. "We've got that."

"I hear a 'but'."

"Landings aren't what they used to be. Codfish are gone, shrimp are almost gone, scallops and urchins are a fraction of what they once were and they can only be taken three months out of the year. Lobsters are doing well but that makes us dependent on a single species."

"So the future's not in fishing?"

I spotted Jake coming through the door, followed by Judith Woods. "I didn't say that." I eyed the two as they approached the bar. "Don't go getting me in trouble." Judith was one of the town's selectmen, and could always be depended on to express her opinion.

"Hey, guys," I said. "Meet Lisa from Pennsylvania."

"Welcome to Flagg's Point," said Jake, sticking out his hand. "Lisa from Pennsylvania…" He looked across at her. "You staying in town with us sea-rats, are ye?"

She laughed, accepting Jake's hand. "I'm here most of the summer."

Judith, it seemed, was in no mood for small talk. "You guys hear the latest?" She held up a finger for her usual, a gin and tonic.

"Hear about what," Jake asked. Lisa remained quiet, but from her eyes it was clear she was paying close attention. So was Annie.

"They decided not to come here."

"The fish packing plant?" I asked. "Thought they were hot for that place down on the wharf."

"So did we," she said, frowning. "We even offered 'em a friggin' tax break."

"They going someplace 'round here?" asked Jake. He'd already started gearing up his boat for what they had said they were planning to buy.

"Hunnerd thirty miles downcoast. Rockport."

"Did they say why?" I asked.

"Closer to the interstate. The boats'll go to them, they say, but they still have to pay the freight to Portland and Boston."

Jake turned away, looking out across the channel, slumping down on the stool. "If I gotta haul my catch all the way down Rockport, all the profit goes in'ta the fuel tank. Them boats down there, they're gonna suck up all *that* business."

"What's this now?" I asked. "The third time?"

"Third in a year," Judith snarled, turning to the bar. "Town can't get a friggin' break."

"Fucking bastards," Jake grumbled. "How the hell can we win?"

"The other two," I ventured. "The marine store and…?"

"The boatyard," Judith replied. "My grandfather used to build boats here, so'd *his* father. But nobody'll touch us now."

"Remind me," I said. "Did either say why they won't come?"

"Marine store said not enough customers here, went to Machiasport. The other idiots just went away."

Adam Russell came in, followed by couple more fishermen, all three wearing big rubber boots and torn jeans. They grabbed beers and headed out back to the deck overlooking the channel. Judith let out a deep sigh and went to join them. When Jake headed over to the pool table he left Lisa and me alone at the bar.

"I don't get it," she said. "Everything they're talking about has to do with fishing." She paused for a sip of wine. "I come here as a visitor, my husband and I are at the big B & B on the hill, Marilyn St. Claire's place. She's booked through the fall and the guests are all spending money. The people who work there all live around here. This town has more to offer than just fishing."

"I know that," I replied, glancing out at the deck. "Careful saying that to *those* guys."

"Cruise ships," she mused. "Lots go into Bar Harbor, why none here?"

"Over there," I pointed towards Eastport, "they have the water and the wharf, but they still don't come. Here, they couldn't get in if they wanted to. And if they did find some way to get people ashore, they'd swamp the town."

She looked up when we heard the sound of raised voices from outside. One of the men was shaking his finger in Judith's face but she wasn't letting up despite the way he towered over her. Instead, she bore in on the man, looking him straight on. When he turned away and backed off, she headed inside towards where Lisa and I sat. We heard the other men laughing.

"Refill my drink, would'ja sweetie?" She passed the empty glass over to Annie and sat down next to Lisa, laughing. "You see all them seals out in the channel?" She chuckled, then added, "putting on a real show out there today."

* * * * *

Annie had been advertising the event for several weeks, even posting it on the local TV cable-loop. Billed as the "Spring Palooza," it offered a potpourri of regional musical talent. From the country-twanged sound to a group that specialized in sea shanteys, it was a

Saturday afternoon and evening of live acts all crammed into the corner of the town's only bar, and all to celebrate the end of winter and beginning of the lobster season. Evelyn and I had marked it on the calendar when it was announced. Everybody I knew was looking forward to the end of a long, dreary winter, even if the event came a month after the last of the snows were gone.

We got there about seven and had to walk two blocks for parking. People spilled out into the street and the voice of a singer rolled through the door, backed by a band with a heavy bass note and an enthusiastic drummer. I followed Evelyn around to the rear and we climbed the back stairs onto the deck.

Inside, the band filled the space near the big mural and a knot of fishermen crowded one end of the bar. At the other end, Judith struggled to hold a conversation with Lisa while both of their men-folk chalked up cue sticks. Annie spotted Evelyn first then me and we got our drinks pretty quickly – she had four staff working behind the bar and all were hustling. There was no shortage of people to talk to, including some who'd made themselves scarce since last fall. You could talk, that is, if your words were not drowned out by the clamor.

The singer belted out a pretty good version of *Me and Bobby McGee* then the bass player emptied the tips bucket and they moved aside for the next act, a guitar duo.

I knew these guys. They had played locally for a long time and never passed up doing a benefit, usually gratis. One had a backwoods beard and the other was clean-shaven and had a laughing face. With these two, you never knew which would take the lead in any particular song – they passed it back and forth freely and sometimes several times in the same piece.

Conversation was difficult, but probably unnecessary. The pair took half a minute to tune their guitars then launched into *Sloop John B*, with the smiling-face reaching effortlessly to the high notes. I stepped over to the bar to refresh our drinks, and by the time I got back to the table Keisha was huddled with Evelyn, their words drowned by the music.

Half the people in the bar and most of those in the street knew the lyrics well enough to join in, even those who had been there more hours than they might confess. With the final notes dying down, I spotted Lisa stepping over to the microphone. It was obvious, the way the clean-shaven one handed over the mic, that something had been rehearsed.

The duo opened to the first notes of *Jar of Hearts* and Lisa looked around the room, waiting for the exact point to start. When she wailed out *"who do you think you are,"* most of the conversation stopped.

Buster Loman stood at the end of the bar, slack-jawed, watching Lisa. His wife Susan stood nearby, watching him. When the closing notes sounded and Lisa returned the mic to its stand, the two Lomans embraced then the musicians started with *Runaway*. Buster and Susan moved to the floor, followed by most of the crowd, stopping only to join in on the *"why – why – why"* refrain, delivered in a high-pitched falsetto by the beard.

I looked around the room for Evelyn but didn't at first spot her. When she burst out into the middle of the room, dancing with Jake, I knew we were in for it. She was always the dancer and apparently was not about to wait for me.

Before I could break in, my arm was grabbed and I was dragged, half-hopping backwards, to the middle of the floor. In the confusion and the dim light with swirling figures gyrating all around us, it was only with difficulty I saw that my partner was Judith. Greg, her husband, was stepping it off with Annie, who had abandoned the bar momentarily to the charge of her employees.

The band was relentless. From *Twist And Shout* to *Only Sixteen* then on to *Dance, Little Sister* but with not even a quarter-note separation, they wouldn't let up. When they got to *Johnny B. Goode* the bedlam was complete. The volume was such that the police might have taken notice, except the sheriff himself was out on the floor attempting to do the twist with a woman three inches taller. Somebody switched on the disco-ball, sending colored specks of light bouncing across the walls and dancers alike.

At one point I backed into another dancer. A sideways glance showed it was Jake, this time paired up with Keisha. Clearly, her twenty-five year advantage was showing. She looked like she had just started, but he was about done for. I'm not sure how many women I danced with, but was relieved to find that when they finally hit a slow piece it was Evelyn that shared it with me.

"We're gonna take us a little break," announced the beard. The room let out a collective sigh of relief, but it was not likely to last long. Off on the side another group had already begun setting up.

I don't know what time it was when Evelyn collapsed into my arms, letting me know it was time to go.

"What's this," I said to her, leaning in close so she could hear. "You're the one calling 'Uncle,' already?"

"Don't you dare go rubbing that in," she replied, feigning a frown.

Three more bands were on the line-up, but we had had enough. We followed Buster and Jake and their respective ladies out onto the street but four more revelers came charging in, followed by Adam Russell and his wife Linda.

White Elephants

One or two at a time, people filed into the meeting room at the Town Office, until twenty or so were seated. New England tradition, as well as the Town Charter, called for a Public Hearing before the town could be called to vote on appropriations that had not already been approved by those who voted in the annual Town Business Meeting. It was always a question how many would bother to come out and learn about what was being proposed, out of the twelve hundred or so who could have cared. The actual vote was set for three weeks later. This evening was to give townspeople the chance to listen and then say what they felt, and about eighteen eligible voters sat or mostly stood, clustered at the rear of the room.

While I looked through the information the town had prepared, Jake sat down next to me. "How long," I asked him, "has that place been shut up?"

"At least ten years," he replied. I continued glancing through the paperwork. The town was proposing to buy an unused commercial building, one that had a roof that remained mostly intact, to turn it into something useful. It once included a gas station, but the tanks had long ago been removed, leaving it a mixed use dinosaur.

Lisa settled down on my other side, and her husband Mitchell sat next to her. Head Selectman Chester Taylor stepped to the front of the room and noisily cleared his throat. "I want to thank you all for coming out tonight," he rumbled, looking around the room. His disappointment at the small turnout was apparent. He shrugged, turned to the display easel, and pulled back the cover page.

"Everybody here knows this place," he said. "At this point it is nothing but a public nuisance, but since the owner's kept his taxes up there's nothing we can do. We need to do something, so we are proposing to make an offer to buy it for the town. He has told me he would accept what we are hoping the town will authorize."

He was right, we all knew the place, just a block from the park that announced the entry to the village. It had been acquired by an out-of-towner some years back, and he'd done nothing with it. Nobody knew why the guy bought it, but everybody knew it was sitting empty and ugly with weeds in the parking lot and rodents wandering the halls. Years earlier it had housed things including a convenience store, car wash, and a laundromat.

"We want to renovate the back part, the old shop, for musical and theatrical events." He flipped the page and showed what it might look like. "The front part, we want to make that into a community center, and the land can be used for public gardens." So far, nobody had raised their hand. "With the subsidized housing right across the street, we believe many of the residents would try their hand at growing things. Also, it'll give our local artists another place to show their work."

"Chester, what's this little idea of yours gonna set us back?" When I turned to look I spotted Buster Loman standing with his arms clenched across his chest and his chin thrust defiantly forward. Susan sat next to him, stony-faced.

"About three hundred thousand." Taylor returned the scowl, then continued. "Buster, you got a better idea what we can do with this place?"

The response came without a pause. "Yeah, I do. Joint's a mess, a freak'n white elephant. Let it fall down. Take that money and give us a new pier. That's what the fishermen need and that's what you should do."

Lisa leaned over and asked me, quiet-like, "who is this man?"

"One of our fishermen," I told her. "Goes out lobstering in the summer, drags for scallops and urchins in the winter. Sometimes does a bit of carpentry work."

"You guys got a new pier just three years ago," Taylor shot back. "Time now to help improve the town."

Adam Russell stood up. Without waiting to be recognized by the chair, he turned towards Buster. "Chet's right," he shouted out. "We don't do something with that place, it's just one more step backwards."

"Backwards my ass! This is bull-shit!" Loman shouted back. "We're a fishing village, and that's all we're *ever* gonna be." He rose and turned toward the door, dragging an unhappy-looking Susan behind him. "We ain't gonna let *nobody* turn this town in'ta no Bah Hahbah." When the door slammed behind the two Lomans, Russell grimaced and sat back down.

Taylor continued with his presentation as though he had not been challenged. He had it all thought out, but was looking for input on other uses. And for the town to support his idea, come the vote in three weeks.

"Chet," came another question, this time from a man wearing a string tie and brandishing the latest Town Report. "This expenditure is not in the budget. How do you propose we finance that three hundred thousand?"

"Thank you, George. I'm suggesting we take out a bond issued through the state. Fifteen years at today's rate will cost us about twenty eight thou each year."

"So what's that mean to my taxes?"

"For a property valued at one hundred thousand, less than a dollar a month."

Lisa leaned over again. "Is that for real?"

"Not sure he can do what he says for that," I replied, "but if he can, I'm sure Chester's checked out the tax angle."

"But George," Taylor continued, thrusting his finger forward, "don't just think of the cost. Think of the benefit. We turn what every one of us sees as an eyesore, maybe even a dangerous one, into a town asset that benefits us all."

"These musical and theatrical events. Who's going to do them?"

"Several groups have expressed interest, and there's a number of performance companies itching for a stage."

"That kind of stuff would really help us extend the season." This time it was Marilyn St. Claire speaking. "We're fully booked June through August," she added. "But in the spring and fall we have a lot of empty rooms."

"Marilyn," replied Taylor, "I'm happy you see it that way."

Lisa leaned over again. "Her place, that's where we've been staying."

"Jake," called out Taylor. "What do you think?"

"I heard tell some folks come here for the seafood," he drawled. "So maybe, the more people in town…" He stood stroking his chin like he was thinking of each word. "The more seafood they're gonna want. Better for all of us we sell our catch local."

By the time the remaining sixteen voters left, it was clear that Taylor had generated some support. The conversation continued out in the parking lot.

"Think he can really do it?" asked one.

"If he can buy it right, 'spect so," said another.

"I, for one," said a third, "am tired of looking at that place like it is now. Back when McGregor ran it he kept it looking real good. Sure ain't that way these days."

"When folks come into town," Jake pointed out, "first thing they see. What's that they say 'bout first impressions?"

Russell came out followed by a nodding Taylor, apparently agreeing with something he had just heard.

* * * * *

It was purely by chance I ran into Adam Russell in the Post Office a week later.

"Arnie," he said while we dug through our respective boxes, "What're you thinking about the town's idea, buying up that old place?"

"Personally, I think it's a good one, if they do it right."

"Yeah," he said. It was obvious he'd been thinking hard about this. "If they do it right."

"Sounds like you're not so sure they can." Truth be told, I was concerned about the same thing – that Taylor might try to do something on the cheap and leave the town stuck with both the debt and the white elephant. He'd be up for reelection in a year, might finally decide it was time to see more of his grand-kids and let someone else finish what he'd started.

"I think the idea's a good one too." He stood in the door, preparing to get on with the day. "Who do you think we can we get, make it work?"

Marilyn St. Claire came to mind as one with the vision, but she'd still need an architect. "Maybe," I said, "we're getting ahead of ourselves here."

"While we're at it," he continued, "can't we do something about those crumbling buildings down on Front Street?" He pointed across the parking lot at one, a long vacant canning plant.

"I hear the board's planning to propose some kind of ordinance. There's going to be a Public Hearing on that."

"Took 'em a while. Something put a bug in their butt?"

"Yeah," I said. "That last windstorm we had, attic window in that one place spilled broken glass over the sidewalk and the street. Damn lucky nobody got hit, some of those shards were pretty big."

"Can't remember when somebody last used that place. Time was, it was pretty nice."

"Not the only place falling down. How 'bout that old warehouse down on the point, shedding all that debris into the water?"

"Don't get me going on that." Adam screwed his face up into an expression of disgust. "Damn tough dodging all that shit in the channel. Could'a wrecked my prop. We gotta do something."

I sat in the parking lot for a couple minutes, just looking out at the channel. One of the buildings, right in plain view, had already lost big chunks and more was ready to go, just waiting for the next big wind. Several of the historical buildings had already been lost, floated off when winds pushed up higher than usual tides, ending up collapsed in a cove on the other side of the channel.

* * * * *

The annual marathon is always a big deal. It brings contestants from as far as California and a number of European countries, all looking forward to participating in one of the very few truly international events. This was to be the fifth running, and it was always timed for the end of June when temperatures in Flagg's Point might still be sufficiently benign for such an event. They'd run from the lighthouse over near Sail Rock, across the bridge and through customs to the lighthouse at the north end of the Canadian island, then cross back again to US soil and the finish line on Front Street, passing through town where the cheering crowd awaited, many drinking the jolly beer served up locally.

Between the runners, their friends, and their family members, nearly two thousand people crowded into town. Residents had learned, from earlier events, that the crush would be short lived but that the restaurants and lodging houses would be swamped. As far off as Calais there was not a bed to be booked for that weekend – all had been reserved by the previous November.

The leaders streaked across the finish line before ten-thirty, then the parade built while the clock continued to run. My job was to interview the front-runners for the paper, but by eleven I was ready for some of that beer.

It was elbow-to-elbow at Annie's Place, even without a band. From the door to the bar took me five minutes, but then Keisha spotted me in the crowd and drew a draft. She and Blondie were both working behind the bar, as well as Annie and two of her regulars, and all were hustling. I spotted several visitors wistfully eyeing the pool table, but with the crowd flowing around all four sides there'd be no way anybody could wield a cue stick. Looking around, I realized I may have been the only local to brave the mob, but Annie was moving beer. Blondie emptied the tips jar twice during the time I was there, and each time it was full.

On my way to the deck I was bumped from behind and turned to look. The man was a bit on the stocky side, didn't look like a runner. He seemed friendly and immediately apologized for his clumsiness.

"Where you here from?" I asked him.

"North Carolina," he replied, hoisting his beer. "I'm not a runner," he added. "That'd be my wife. She's nuts but that's okay with me."

"All right," I laughed. "My wife's nuts too."

"She a runner?"

"No," I said. "She paints."

"Hey, brother! I feel your pain!" He gave me a high-five then turned to point out at the channel where a flock of hungry cormorants dove for their supper. "You live here?"

"I do," I told him. "Ten years now, still a newbie."

"Is it always this crowded around here?"

"No," I reassured him. "Marathon brings out the crowd. Where're you staying?"

"We got lucky," he said. "Motel over there had a cancellation." He pointed across the channel to where the Canadian flag fluttered in the breeze. "We're already planning to come back when it's not so crazy. Never knew about this place before now."

"What'd you see?"

"Yesterday, we did the trails over by the lighthouse. Never saw nothing like that before." He glanced at his watch. "Hey, gotta go," he laughed, waving a camera. "Miss getting a shot of her coming across the line, I'm in deep shit."

Heading back onto the street, I saw that the restaurants had lines out on the sidewalk and the street vendors, in for the day, were busy despite the fact that many runners wouldn't be off the course for another hour or so. I guessed my new friend's wife had done this before so he knew just when to be on his toes.

By the evening, the main drag through town was open, the vendors packed up, and most of the visitors had moved on. The town breathed a sigh of relief and prepared to get on where they had left off forty-eight hours earlier. Other events remained on the calendar, but the next marathon was a year away.

* * * * *

The town anticipated there'd be a bigger turnout than before, so the Public Meeting on Chester's pet project three weeks later was held in the fire bay. Even so, judging from the expressions on the faces of the selectmen, the number registering to vote on the referendum question was a surprise, easily topping a hundred a full twenty minutes before the gavel went down.

The Select Board sat behind the table at the front, facing the crowd. Chester Taylor took the seat nearest the center, and Judith was on the opposite end. An array of posters had been put up behind the table, showing artists renderings, engineering plans, and blown-up spreadsheets.

36

The first step, electing a moderator, took only a few minutes then the presentation began.

"Three weeks ago," said Taylor, "at the public hearing we got a strong positive response from our residents." A low grumble came from the left side, back at the rear. I spotted Buster Loman, surrounded by a large contingent of fishermen and older residents. Taylor's face was crestfallen but he managed to hide what he must have been thinking.

Over to my right I overheard Marilyn speaking to a friend. "I haven't missed a business meeting since I came to town," she said. "Don't ever remember seeing *that* crowd come in."

The moderator, following the way such things are done, read the article then called out, "Do I hear a motion that this article be accepted as written?" Several hands went up and the clerk recorded two names. Then, "is there any discussion?"

It was only with prolonged pounding of the gavel that the room was silenced. Shout after shout had come from the left rear, all demanding to be heard. One rose and stood silently, looking defiantly at the moderator and waiting to be recognized.

"Mr. Ashley," said the moderator. "You have the floor."

"Mr. Moderator," the man began. "I am opposed to this plan because it will raise taxes and provide no benefit to a large number of us who have lived here all our lives including some on limited income. Also, Mr. Taylor didn't mention that purchasing this property will take better than forty-four thousand off the tax rolls. It won't cost us the twenty-eight thousand each year like he said, it'll be closer to thirty-three thousand. There are other things this town needs more than to own a white elephant."

Again, the moderator pounded the gavel to restore order.

Marilyn St. Claire stood tall, over on the right side. The moderator nodded to her. "This town has a lot to offer," she said. "That's why people come here, and that's why people want to come back. This is an opportunity to give them one more reason to visit, and give the people of the town something too."

"Yeah," called out a voice from the left. "It'll give us something more we gotta pay for."

More gavel pounding, and the crowd again fell silent. "Anybody else?" asked the moderator. A few more from both sides rose to speak but the arguments were the same. The room fell into a tense silence with both sides hurling dagger-eyes across the room.

The moderator stood at the podium, scanning the room but looking like he'd prefer being anywhere else. "Hearing nothing more, we are now going to vote on this. It will be by written ballot."

The line snaked around the room and – for the most part – those waiting to vote were polite and restrained. I saw that many had figured out where the like-minded stood and drifted towards that spot as if they were seeking refuge from a fight.

Half an hour later, the moderator called out: "Has everybody voted who wants to?" When no more stood, he gestured to the clerk to open the box and count the ballots. A deathly silence prevailed while the slips of paper were divided into two piles and counted, re-counted, cross-checked, and re-cross-checked. Ten minutes later, the clerk handed a piece of paper to the moderator.

"Thirty-four people have voted to accept this proposal," he called out. "And one hundred and eleven have voted to reject it. The 'Nays' have it, the article fails. Do I hear a motion to adjourn?"

Several tight knots of people clustered in the parking lot. I spotted Marilyn with a group of her friends and joined in. "It's the damn phone tree again," one said. "Just a few calls, they can drag out their buddies and pack the place."

"Yeah," said another, "a hundred and forty-five votes cast. Around here, that's a lot."

"How can it be a lot? That's way less than twenty percent of the voters."

"How many of these have you been to? Lot'sa times they can't even get a quorum."

"How many's that?"

"Twenty-five. A measly twenty-five voters, all it takes."

An hour later I drifted over to the bar, looking for a quiet beer and maybe a friendly word. It didn't take long to realize I'd find neither, as soon as I spotted Buster Loman on the porch with a cluster of people gathered around.

"This is our friggin town too," I heard him say before the crowd noise drowned him out. That was when Lisa came in and ordered her usual glass of wine.

"I heard it got shot down." She glanced at the crowd on the deck. "Marilyn St. Claire's some kind'a bummed out. She thought it'd be great for the town."

"So did I," I replied, gesturing with my thumb towards the deck. "You want another point of view? Look no further."

"What's their objection?"

"Probably each'd give a different answer," I shrugged. "I think it's a control thing." She looked at me like she thought I was being evasive. "Four out of the five members of the current Select

Board didn't go to High School here. Some of these guys resent what they see as 'outside interference'."

"So why don't some of them run for office?"

"You have any idea how many people ask that question?"

* * * * *

The tradition went back many years, I was told. To mark the end of the school year and the beginning of the summer, when many of the kids would head out on fishing boats or pull on the big rubber boots and hit the clam flats, Judith and her husband Greg hosted a big barbecue. Much of the food was donated by the local stores, but it was a poorly kept secret that the two funded the balance. A few townspeople would bring in big bags of chips or tubs of potato salad, but neither ever asked for money.

By the time I got there Greg and Buster were half-concealed in swirling clouds of pungent smoke, carefully tending rows of sausages and hamburgers and hot dogs, sending platter after platter to the ravenous crowd. Three grilles had flames dancing above sizzling meat, and a fourth was busy toasting the rolls.

"Hey Arnie!" Greg grabbed my arm and dragged me into the smoke. "Look after these for me, just a minute okay?" Before I could respond he was gone and I had a long-handled fork in my hand. I spotted him carrying a huge tray towards the table where hungry kids, parents, and grand-parents were lined up.

Buster laughed when a burst of flame leapt up at me from the sausages I had attempted to turn. "Din't know you was gonna go home smelling like pork smoke, did'ja!"

"How many of these you guys got going?"

"Nuff to fill two hunnerd bellies." The smoke momentarily engulfed him – by the time it cleared he too had dragged off a platter and Greg was standing in his place.

Judith appeared next to me. "I see you let yerself get shanghaied."

"Whaddaya mean," I protested. "You guys were trying to hog all the fun."

"Here," said Buster, handing me a juicy hamburger. "Gotta take care o' the help."

I hadn't noticed Jake and Marlene standing in line, but apparently Buster did. He called Judith over and handed her a plate with two burgers. "This' how he likes it done," he said, pointing at Jake. "Take this over, okay?"

Most of an hour later the line dwindled down to those few looking for seconds – or maybe thirds. "Arnie, you're a dear for helpin' out," said Judith, bustling past with a tub full of pickle relish. "You get yourself somethin' to eat?"

I pulled the last of the sausages off and dumped them on the platter. "You're kidding, right?" After three burgers and a big sausage sandwich laden with sautéed onion, I wasn't sure I'd be ready for dinner later on. "Anybody ever go away from one of these hungry?"

"Not if we got anything say 'bout it." She laughed and headed back to start the clean-up. "Make sure you take some o' this stuff home to Evelyn, ya hear?"

* * * * *

A group of kids, maybe five six year olds, went dashing past me as I stood browsing in the library, all headed for the community room. Glancing through the door, the room was full of rioting party-goers and Blondie was right in the middle of it, with several other parents standing timorously along the edges of the tumult.

"Birthday party," observed Melinda, the librarian. "She had no other place so we're showing them a movie." Three more, all gaily dressed, noisily shoved past me like I wasn't there.

"Cool," I said. "What movie?"

"A Johnny Depp movie. *Charlie and the Chocolate Factory.*"

Not having seen that movie, particularly in the company of a crowd of rowdy six year olds, I decided to stick around for a few minutes. Evelyn was out of town doing a show in Baltimore and nobody expected anything of me that day.

I had already heard the story of how Blondie, who was rarely called by her real name Doris Carson, had become a teen-mother but somehow still managed to finish high school, and was firmly determined that her daughter Clarissa would also graduate. Her own family had fully accepted her child, unlike that of the child's father, who had left town years earlier.

"Disappeared in the middle o'the night, he did," said Jake, who had had his eye on him as a potential crew member. Blondie herself had lost her own father, when the lobsterman *MaryLou* went down in a nasty storm eight years earlier, along with three other men.

The kids settled down when the movie opened. Soon I found myself sucked into the plight of Charlie's father, Mr. Bucket, employed by a toothpaste factory to screw the cap on each tube as the conveyer belt carried it by. When his job is taken over by a robot, the family is plunged deeper into poverty, yet they remain cheerful and dedicated to each other.

Blondie sat in the middle of the room with Clarissa on her lap, surrounded closely by a sea of pink. She knew I was there but paid no attention – it was clear who she was there for. Another group formed up in the back, all boys, one of whom was Buster Loman's grandson.

The story unfolded, showing how Charlie acquired one of only five tickets for a special tour of the nearby chocolate factory, long shuttered but now reopened, where his bedridden grandfather had once worked. One of the five was promised a mysterious 'Grand Prize' to be awarded after the tour. The tale was interspersed with images of Mr. Bucket with his nose buried deep in textbooks, with no clue given as to what he was studying.

Looking around the room, as the story continued all eyes were glued to the screen. Charlie, it turned out, of the five kids on the tour was the only one you might want to claim as your own. The others are greedy, boastful, clumsy, or all three. When one is turned into a giant blueberry, another nearly drowns in a river of chocolate, and the third is shrunk to just a few inches the party-goers break into laughter and cheers.

At the conclusion, Charlie is offered the promised Grand Prize: to become heir to the factory. He turns it down when told he must leave his family behind, just as Willy Wonka – the owner – left his own. Willy's childhood, it turns out, was dysfunctional and he ultimately left his father, a sadistic dentist.

Blondie, however, appeared to have been drawn deeply into the story of Mr. Bucket's embrace of education. In a concluding scene he is awarded the position of maintaining the machines that had earlier taken his job. Thanks to his studies, he claimed a better spot than the one he'd lost – one that modern industry needed to have filled. Blondie sat chewing on her lip, locked onto that portion of the story, apparently taking in how Mr. Bucket had engineered his own reversal of fortune.

The cake was brought in just when the credits began to roll. Melinda offered me a slice but I declined. I was having too much fun simply watching the kids.

* * * * *

The mood was ugly before the Public Hearing even started, what with all the muttering from the back seats. The Select Board had called it to talk about the Dangerous Building Ordinance they were proposing, intended to deal with the crumbling buildings mostly along Front Street.

"We all know where these places are," Chet said opening the meeting. "That last storm blew out two attic windows. Broken glass in the street is bad enough but that's only the start. We know that kids go in some of them and if they get hurt we're all on the hook because we've been ignoring the problem. The way it is right now..." He looked around the room at the thirty or so gathered in front of him and the other board members. "Only if the owners stop paying taxes can we can seize these properties and do something about it. If they stay current, for us it's hand's off."

"You can't make them clean it up, make it safe?" asked one. I recognized him as a friend of Buster who usually agreed with everything he said.

"Not without an ordinance," replied Chester. "It won't stand up in court unless we have something in place that we all live by. That's why we're asking the town to support this." He waved a small

44

sheaf of papers, similar to those in a stack by the door. "To pass this," he added, "we will need to have a referendum."

A man in the second row asked "Who in here has read this?" A smattering of hands went up.

"It's been available here in the office for two weeks, like the posting said." Chester's expression had switched from confident to alarmed.

"We've talked about this before," called out another. "A bad idea then, a bad idea now."

"That's what I say too." This time it was a woman, standing off to the right with a defiant glare. I recognized her as the wife of one of the fishermen. "Bad enuff we got pushed back from the waterfront where we always used to live. Now these guys want to tell us what color we can paint our shed."

"Now wait a minute Lilianne!" I had never heard Chester sound angry before. "That's not at all what this says." He waved the paper like he would throw it at her, but she stood with her arms over her chest and her jaw stuck out.

"Maybe it don't say that now," she shouted back. "This gets passed, soon 'nuff it will!"

"She's right," growled another. "This here idea's a slippery slope. Once it gets started who knows where it's going. I don't want you guys turn this town into another Bah Hahbah an' tell me what I kin do with my own property." He jabbed his finger towards the ceiling. "I say let these places fall int'a the sea."

I turned to my neighbor and said quietly, "several already have."

"Yes," he whispered back. "And her place is prob'ly next."

"You get this going," said a third, "gonna hurt folks got nothing. Turn 'em outa their homes because they can't patch up their porches."

"Some of our people poor as Job's turkey," called out a man from the rear. "This ain't gonna help *them* none."

Chester sat at the front, crestfallen. Judith looked around the room, but said nothing. The other members of the board looked like they wanted to be anywhere else.

"That last idea of yours weren't so great," called out a man standing over on the left near the door wearing big rubber boots. "See how many people come out to vote on *this* one."

The crowd broke into a general uproar and people started heading for the exit. Soon the meeting room was empty. I headed for home; Annie's maybe wasn't the place to visit this evening.

<u>Helicopters</u>

As inevitably as the weeds in the garden, the school budget referendum comes around every August, before the town calculates the taxes to be levied on property owners. The subject is dry and detail-oriented, much less fun than lounging in the back yard watching the laundry dry. In Flagg's Point it also accounts for somewhat more than half of the town's annual budget, and the yearly process had been covered by the local paper in tedious detail.

When the superintendent stepped to the microphone, eighteen people stopped talking and turned to hear what he had to say.

"I'm afraid I don't have a whole lot of good news to share with you folks tonight," he said by way of openers. "Your school board has done the hard work of flat-lining the operating budget. Some costs have been cut way down, many have stayed at last year's level, and only a few have increased. Overall, the actual cost of educating our students has decreased from last year. That's the good news."

Eighteen people shifted nervously, leaning forward so's not to miss the punch line.

"Thanks to the school funding formula given us by the legislature, state support of the Flagg's Point school has also been cut way back." He waved a copy of the proposed budget. "I hope you all have a copy of this. Look on page one where it says 'Educational Subsidy'."

Papers rustled all over the room.

"The state's contribution was reduced last year, and it's been cut again this year." The formula, he described in the driest of detail, is based largely on miles of shoreline within the town, based on the legislative assumption that in Maine that is the principal driver of real estate value. By that measure Flagg's Point was wealthy indeed – no matter that well over eighty percent of the town's students qualified for subsidized meals. We all knew that some of the bigger and wealthier school districts were in towns with no shoreline at all, leading them to claim the dollars we lost. They also had more votes in the legislature.

"Still on page one, look at the line titled 'Total Local Taxes.' It's gone up more than ten percent for this next year. Even if the overall cost is down, it still must be covered."

He looked around the room, responding to the scattered groans, then added "for a property worth one hundred thousand dollars, that's an increase of nearly four dollars per month."

From that point on it was a matter of pointing out various budget lines and answering questions – most of which were perfunctory.

"Any comments?" he asked.

One of the older residents stuck up his hand. "Every year the school budget goes up." A muted grumble rolled around the room. "When will it stop?"

"If it keeps going the way it's going right now," the Superintendent replied, "in another year or so all of the state subsidies will drop to zero. That's when it will stop. They can't give us less than nothing."

Marilyn rose and identified herself. "This is what we need so we can educate the children of the town, right?"

"It's about as good as you're going to see," he replied.

"Can we thank our governor for this?"

The supe drew a deep breath, closed his eyes, and clenched his lips.

"Okay," Marilyn said. "I get it."

The vote was by a show of hands and passed unanimously. The entire process took twenty minutes and created no arguments. Afterwards, out in the parking lot people greeted each other warmly then went home.

* * * * *

That Saturday evening I stopped by the bar again. Over on one side Judith Woods was trying to enjoy her gin and tonic while Buster was doing all he could to disrupt her leisure. Lisa sat back, pretending to not listen. Nearby, two men played a good-natured game on the pool table, with neither scoring very many shots. Jason Williams' sweatshirt was emblazoned with *F/V Mary Lynne* and Roger Helman's read *Wade's Wire Traps*. The two were often seen together – they both crewed on Adam Russell's boat. Jake once told me they were a standout duo on the high school basketball team and that neighboring coaches were very glad to see them graduate.

"Two in the corner," Jason called out.

A few seconds later Roger laughed. "I heard what you done called," he guffawed. "Nine in the side, right?"

"Gimme a break," grumbled Jason. "Least I got *something* in."

Lisa nudged my elbow to get my attention, then pointed at Jason and Roger. "What is it with the big rubber boots?" She paused

49

for a sip of wine, then pointed at several other men with similar footgear. "Is this a guy thing around here?"

I laughed at her question. "I've heard tell, you aren't the only one asking that." She gave me a puzzled look. "Some of the young women have complained they can't get the guys take off those boots even..."

"Don't say it. During romantic interludes."

"Yeah. Even then."

"Yeah," interjected Annie, apparently listening in. "Specially then."

We all laughed. When I turned back to see what Buster had on his mind, Lisa tossed down a few bills and headed for the door.

"How 'kin you guys be doing that?" he asked Judith. "Raise our taxes like that without even letting us have a say-so? What'd you guys go and buy?"

"That wasn't us," she protested. "We done held the line. It's all in the school budget."

"When I was a kid in that school," he said, pushing a finger into her face, "we din't have no gold-plated desks or nothing. Din't even have no busses."

"Cut the crap, Buster." Judith angrily shoved his finger aside and stood in front of him glowering. She was six inches shorter and lacked the build of one who labored at sea, but stood with shoulders square and hands on hips. "Your folks place was right on South Street like two blocks from the friggin school. And you wouldn't have gotten on that damn bus even if it stopped for you."

Apparently realizing he was getting nowhere with her, he turned to me. "Whadda *you* think? Do those kids need what we never got?"

"Were you at the meeting the other night, hear what the supe had to say?"

"What meeting?"

"The school budget referendum. It was posted all over town."

"So now you're gonna throw all kind 'a numbers at me?"

"Nope," I said, taking a swig of beer. "Learning about the numbers, that's *your* job."

"Who the hell's got time for that?"

"Spect that's so," I replied. "Just like that place Chester Taylor wanted us to buy."

"That's 'bout as harebrained as anything I *ever* seen." He turned and headed out to the deck where the smokers all clustered along the railing.

"Give it up, Arnie." Judith drained the last of her drink. "Guy's always been like that, long's I've known him." She snickered. "He's one could find the devil in a two-dollar bill."

Not wanting to touch that comment, I took the easy way out. "What about that funding formula?"

"That's where the problem is," she said, holding up the empty glass to catch Annie's eye. "They want to fix property taxes, that's what they gotta take care of. Way it's set now, they don't even *look* at household income or all the kids we got on subsidized meals.

Only shoreline footage. Makes us out to be rich as friggin' Camden. They don't even think of all that property in land trusts that don't pay the same taxes like everybody else. Problem is, down Augusta, they like it just fine way it is, don't see there's nothing *needs* to get fixed."

Judith wrinkled up her nose and took the first sip from her fresh glass. "Them bastards down there," she muttered, "they could fuck up a soup sandwich."

Jason and Roger sat down nearby, laughing at how neither could qualify as a pool-shark. "What's her name – the black chick?" asked Jason.

"You mean Keisha?" Roger asked.

"Yeah, that's her. We gotta both keep our distance if *she's* pack'n a cue stick."

When Judith laughed out loud, "that one, she's a hot number all right," they both sat back grinning like they'd already been fleeced.

"Speakin' o' hot numbers…" Jason turned to Roger. "Haven't seen much o' your daughter lately."

"Tiffy's got a lot going on," laughed Roger, holding up his empty mug for a refill. "Maybe after basketball tournaments get done we can all get together like we did last year."

"I'd like that." Jason upended his mug and gestured for more. "Bethany's been askin'. That was a good lot of fun." He took a swig from the fresh mug and looked over at Roger. "Think the team'll get a fire truck escort back to town this year?"

"Dunnow," Roger replied. "They been doin' a lot of winning this year."

* * * * *

A few days later I found myself at Annie's Place again, this time alongside Jake, just the two of us.

"I know *you're* paying attention to this crap." He pointed down to the day's newspaper with the latest headline showing. "Mebbe I should'a looked closer back in September."

"Tell you what," I said. 'If you had told me, two weeks ago, that a senior member of the White House staff would be on national television hawking shoes for one of the president's family members, I would have laughed at you."

"Don't seem so funny now." He took a deep breath and looked out across the channel where the Canadian flag beckoned in the breeze. "How'd we get here?"

"Don't know." I drained my beer and gestured to Annie for a refill. "Don't know where this is taking us, either."

"That governor of ours, now he thinks he can get away with anything he wants. That's what that new guy down Washington has convinced him."

I took a sip of beer and considered the state of things. "That guy in Washington, I don't think he's an *evil* man. I think he's a *weak* man. He doesn't see he's allowed himself to be surrounded by jerks out to manipulate him, bad guys each with their own agenda. Look at it this way, Jake. He's asked some pretty sharp guys to help him, been turned down by a bunch. It's only the loser's will work for him, and not even enough of *them*. How long could you keep your boat going with a crew like that?"

"Be on the rocks in a week," he groaned. "Least I know I c'n trust who's steering when I'm away from the wheel."

"You guys bitching again?" I turned to see Judith standing behind us, hands on hips. "What the hell's it this time?"

"Oh, you know. Same old same old. Nothing's new."

"You wanna know what I think?" she asked.

"What *you* think?" I turned to face her straight-on, with Jake nodding in agreement. "Of course I do."

Judith picked her drink up from the bar and took a sip. "This's what I think. It ain't pretty out there and it's only gonna get worse. I think we need to do more look after ourselves, them jerks in Washington and Augusta ain't gonna be looking to help us way out here. If they had their way we'd just fall off int'a the ocean."

"Okay," drawled Jake. "Whuzzat mean?"

"Think of it this way," she continued. "Why do all those people come here in the summer? Flagg's Point ain't on the way to nowhere. You can go over there…" She pointed across the channel at the Canadian flag, "but once you're there you gotta come back here to go anywhere else. That private ferry they got over there only runs in the summer and don't take very many people, so even then they mostly come back here. What can we do get them to stay a bit longer?"

"You know what Buster'll say to that." Jake sat back with a laugh. "He'll give you the old line. They come to town with a clean shirt and a twenty dollar bill. Four days later they leave, they got a dirty shirt and a twenty dollar bill."

"Something's gonna come along," she said, draining her drink. "Don't know what it'll be, but it'll be something."

* * * * *

The sound started imperceptibly, slowly growing until it rose to the point where it finally got through my skull.

It was helicopters – not one, but two. Both bearing the distinctive red stripe of the Coast Guard. They would only bring a pair of those birds from their Cape Cod roost for one reason: something awful had happened. Watching them pass slowly overhead, heading towards the Grand Manan Channel at an altitude of maybe five hundred feet, my stomach knotted up in fear.

Evelyn heard them too, and came out to watch them clatter across the sky. "What's happening?" she asked.

"Don't know," I replied. "Can't be good." We watched as they vanished beyond the hills to the south.

Down at Annie's Place a cluster of townspeople had gathered around a radio somebody'd brought in. Judith Woods was there, so was Buster Loman and a number of other fishermen. When laughter at the bar erupted, the icy glare from that group was enough to silence anyone. I stepped close to hear what was coming across the airwaves.

It hit me like a falling tree when I heard what it was they were searching for: *Mary Lynne*. Adam Russell and his crew were out there somewhere. A distress call had been received, followed by deadly silence. Nearly five hours of silence.

"Who was on board?" asked one.

55

"His reg'lar crew. Jason and Roger," replied Judith without looking up.

"Jason Williams and Roger Helman," said another. "They been with him couple years."

"Roger's kid's in school here." Judith looked up with tears streaming down her face. "And Jason just got married to Bethany Wilcox couple months ago."

"Do their families know 'bout this?" asked the first.

"They do," replied Judith. "We got people over sittin' with 'em."

"Anything we can do?"

"Got my boat standing by," said Buster, pointing down to the dock. "They get a sighting I be out there real quick, tow him in."

I stepped aside to call Evelyn. "I'll be here until I hear something," I told her after explaining what was happening.

Nobody was buying beers or downing shots or shooting pool. Annie set up a coffee pot and kept it coming, but most of the time the place was deadly silent except for the radio chatter as the helicopter crews coordinated a grid-by-grid search of the area the signal had come from. Every fisherman around knew the area, it was known both for treacherous and unpredictable currents, and also for yielding up a rich bounty for those accepting the risk. And they all understood that risk.

The first sighting was debris only, no sign of a forty-two foot vessel or three men. A life ring with the boat name was spotted just south of Morton Ledge where the depth drops to nearly forty-five fathoms but the in-shore current can hit five knots. The clock stopped and nobody breathed, the only sound was the gurgling of the coffee pot and the occasional disjointed voice crackling over the radio. The crowd had swelled to nearly twenty, and all had the same question: was there to be mourning tonight?

Fundy Bay communities... Nay, all fishing communities, they know this ache: The knowledge that tonight you will sleep between clean sheets, perhaps fitfully, but not far away a new widow weeps, a young mother struggles to tell her children that which can never be fully explained, and family members try to convince each other that life must somehow go on, and surely will. *If there is a just God, how can He allow men to die like this when they are merely trying to feed their families, to fulfil their ordained task in the only world they know?* The gnawing doubt that something has happened comes long before the fatal acceptance that indeed, it has. It is a sudden and numbing sensation: that point at which all hope is surrendered.

An hour or maybe a lifetime later the quiet of the crowded bar was shattered by the raspy but urgent voice coming across the airwaves. *"Mark mark mark."* Every person in the place rushed to hear: *what did they spot, and where?*

In the swirling waters near Sail Rock, the stern of a vessel emerged briefly from the froth, just long enough for one of the helicopter crews to spot the name: *Mary Lynne*. The wreckage disappeared again, likely following the current toward the historic burial ground where depths reach over eighty fathoms; the vessel dragged down by the weight of the four-hundred horsepower Cummins diesel. The sea-bottom outside of the Quoddy Narrows, in the northern end of the Grand Manan Channel, is littered with doomed vessels, some dating from well before 1874 when formal records were first kept.

Despite the momentary sighting, the sea yielded no sign of any of the men, or of other survival gear, and in the late hour hopes were fading as fast as the light.

"I'm going out," said Buster, speaking in a low voice that reeked of finality. "I know them waters. If he's out there I'm bringing them guys home." Several others grabbed foul weather gear and followed him out the door. Soon there was a parade of vessels following *Lobster One* down the narrows, all headed out. In a matter of minutes the harbor was dotted with moored skiffs but the fleet was gone.

I joined with a group driving down to the shore where the trail led along the rocky cliffs favored by visitors. A few carried lights powerful enough to light up the surf crashing eighty feet down, but we saw nothing. Eventually the night went dark and the batteries started giving out. Even though we searched in silence, we all understood that the worst thing for a drowning man would be to struggle to the rocks just to die of exposure with the fifty degree water swirling around his exhausted body and the tangles of rockweed tugging at his ankles. The sorrowful clanging of the bell on the Morton Ledge buoy punctuated our sadness but only made the scene more dismal. Walking in the darkness, feeling our way along the rocky, root-strewn path back to the parking lot, no one spoke. We heard the engines of the fleet just beyond Sail Rock and the stentorian roar of the foghorn, triggered by one of the boats, but heard nothing joyous.

My heart was full when I pulled into our driveway. Tonight, I would sleep in the warm arms of my wife, but three men would sleep in a forest of kelp. I didn't really know either of the crewmen, and barely knew Adam, but tonight my adopted home town had three empty chairs, three dinners lovingly prepared but left uneaten, three wives who would not receive their good-night kiss.

Evelyn greeted me at the door. She had gone down to Annie's and came back with as many details as I had. When I embraced her, standing in the secure cone of light on our porch, I felt her trembling. "Life," she said softly, "carries no guarantees."

Of course, hope as we all did, nobody really expected we would find anything, and in particular anybody alive. Buster and his impromptu crew searched the turbulent waters until low fuel forced their return, following the fleet back to the mooring field. The Coast Guard promised to send one helicopter back the next morning, but now as a recovery operation. Even after the renewed search, we all knew that Adam and his crew, as well as the *Mary Lynne*, had joined that awful list of mariners who were still out working the water, and who would remain there.

The Coast Guard report came a bit later and was inconclusive. There were no weather events to blame the accident on, and even though it happened during daylight hours there were no witnesses. Adam was a skilled and experienced captain who took pride in careful maintenance, and his boat was well equipped with modern electronics. His call was coolly professional, but only sent once and with no information other than the urgency of distress.

Had the *Mary Lynne* been overwhelmed by a rogue wave breaking unexpectedly in the shoal waters near Morton Ledge? Had Adam suffered a heart attack and lost control, losing out to the treacherous currents? Had a foot entanglement taken a man over the stern then the rescue attempt went awry? Guesses, only guesses.

Most of the community gathered in front of the church two days later, and those who could get in filled the pews. There were many tears but no answers. "These men..." The pastor gestured towards the knot of fishermen crowded together, looking uncomfortable on the unfamiliar turf, addressing them in a soft, reassuring voice. "They are the providers. God has assigned them the task of feeding us all, but the sea commands a heavy burden."

It didn't matter how soft the words were; they were sincere and plainspoken but didn't end the ache – three men were still gone. We all returned home after the service, to our own home and hearth, but the void remained.

* * * * *

I never thought I'd see the day when Jake and Buster would embrace, particularly in public, but then that Saturday evening at Annie's Place was not the typical slugfest. Political differences were shoved aside and the niceties of civil conversation abandoned while the community took halting steps towards healing and moving forward. Both men knew, as did many of the others, that it was the hand of fate carelessly tossing the dice that came up with the numbers that determined who would be next, and it could easily be either of them.

"It weren't nothing on his boat took 'em out." Buster stood swirling a glass of Jack Daniels, looking like he'd lost his brother. "Adam was way too careful for that."

"How I see it too," replied Jake. "But I tell you what…" He took a sip from his glass and closed his eyes. A double handful of fishermen stood silently, waiting for him to continue.

"No way I'm gonna end up that old guy just hangin' on, waitin' fer someone come round wipe the drool off a' my chin. That's not hardly what I want." He upended his glass and wiped his mouth on his sleeve. "My time comes, I wanna go out like Adam."

Buster nodded like he agreed but didn't want to say so. "You wanna jist disappear?"

60

"No, that'd be too hard on Marlene, the kids." Jake motioned to Annie for a refill. "They need to have something stick in the ground, get closure. To go like he done..."

"But Jason and Roger?"

"Yeah," said Jake, accepting the fresh glass from Annie. "That's the hell of it. Captain's *first* job bring his crew home. I *know* Adam done died trying."

The crowd fell into silence and the normally cheerful bar became like a morgue, despite the colored lights and the late afternoon sun slanting across the abandoned deck. Blondie slipped in unnoticed and sat on the stool nearest the door, just across from the pool table, now heaped over with casually tossed jackets. Annie spotted her and dropped her elbows onto the surface, just opposite where she sat.

"Too many of these, Annie." Blondie reached over the bar and put her hand on Annie's arm. "Just too many."

"How many's it been since...?"

Blondie took a deep breath and looked up. "Since we lost *my* Daddy?"

Annie made no attempt to reply.

"This is the third one," she continued. "And that's just for us here." A tear trickled down her cheek while she thought of a few more. "Those guys out Grand Manan, they had a few o' their own."

Judith came in and slid silently into the seat next to Blondie, saying nothing. She reached her arm around and pulled the younger woman close, and the trio silently wept.

About that time it got the best of me. I dropped a few bills on the bar and made my way home to Evelyn, feeling like I'd been a voyeur at a stranger's wake.

* * * * *

The long-awaited big game came only a week after the accident and Tiffany Helman was scheduled to play. Now in her final year playing for the Flagg's Point Hornets, as an eighth grader she was strong but not yet one of the star players. Tiffany was known as a scrappy player solid at playing wing and scoring from outside of the paint, not at all reluctant to get in a larger opponent's face and quite aware of the threshold beyond which she'd foul out. To the Calais Blue Devils she was also a known quantity, beyond merely being one who wore a rival uniform: she had scored against them repeatedly in earlier games.

Evelyn and I didn't attend all of the games but when we could, we did. Buster and his friends found seats in the bleachers before we arrived and their presence could not be ignored, what with all the noise they made. Calais came out onto the floor to start warm-up exercises first; their shortest was taller than our tallest. The Hornets came out quickly afterwards and went to work on their warm-up routine. Tiffany, wearing number 42, was right there with them but it was clear her mind was not in the game. No longer a little girl but not yet a woman, she was at that awkward age. She seemed unaware that when she grew into her body, she may easily be one of the most attractive women in town. But tonight there appeared to be only one thing on her mind, and it was not basketball.

What was not clear was whether any of the Blue Devils either recognized her distraction, or knew of its origin.

However, it was apparent that every single Flagg's Point booster shared in her feelings, and doubly so for each of the Hornets.

She was the only player on the floor to have lost her father just a week earlier and probably only those from her side knew it. At the tip-off she got the ball and drove toward the basket but ended up sprawled on the floor before she got halfway there, fouled right at the start.

The crowd yelled loud in encouragement despite her missing both shots, the ball not even hitting the rim. The game progressed with players surging back and forth and both teams scoring equally. The coach could have pulled Tiffany but apparently thought better, preferring to let her work on her anguish out on the court. Maybe he felt some things are more important than continuing a winning streak. I knew who she was, but didn't know her beyond being one of the kids in our town, and had seen just enough to know that her performance tonight was not up to her usual.

When the half-time buzzer sounded both teams retreated to the bench and huddled. Several players rose as substitutes for those who were tiring, but when play resumed number 42 was back out on the floor. The game continued with neither giving any quarter and both obviously flagging. After the third time she scored from a side-angle shot Calais called a time-out. After that it seemed that the Blue Devils had started double-teaming her. I watched one play where a Calais player headed the ball down-court but Tiffany snatched it and fired it off to a teammate, leading to a basket while the opposing player stood befuddled.

With the clock ticking down in the final period, the score stood at 24-22 with Calais leading. They missed a shot with only seven seconds left in the game, and the stands went suddenly silent when the ball ended up in Tiffany's hands. She raced to the middle of the court, leapt high above her Calais defenders, and fired the ball towards the net. A split second after it left her hands, the buzzer sounded and she collapsed to the floor.

All eyes watched the ball soar above the court, a high arching trajectory, moving in slow-motion towards destiny and taking forever to get there. When it passed through the hoop, hardly ruffling the net, the crowd erupted. I don't know how many noted, at least at first, that Tiffany lay in a heap mid-court, sobbing, surrounded by her team-mates. Buster was one of the first to her side, ahead of the coach. She may not have even seen her scoring shot.

We gathered up our things and headed towards the door. Most times the end of a game would be a noisy event with neighbors greeting each other and friendly banter passing freely, but not so this time. Many had tears trickling down and some cried openly. Few spoke and when they did it was in muted tones. Even the Calais boosters recognized that something special had just happened and respected the moment.

Several of the fishermen assisted Mary Ellen Helman, Roger's widow and Tiffany's mother, out to her car. Partially collapsed on strong arms, several burly fishermen helped her to the passenger door then one of their wives stepped around to drive her home. I knew that Mary Ellen and Tiffany would mourn that night, but they would not grieve alone.

* * * * *

By three o'clock the crowd filled the school cafeteria and more were lined up in the parking lot, many bearing pies and cakes for the auction or items to add to the Chinese raffle. If I had to guess, maybe two hundred people were inside before we got there, with more coming along every minute. I recognized many from neighboring towns, and not just those with fishing families. Tables set up in the hallway were already covered with contributions to be sold to benefit the survivors of those lost.

Mary Ellen Helman was not there, nor were any family members of the others who went down with the *Mary Lynne*. They were to be the beneficiaries but with less than three weeks gone by all knew they were not ready yet to be participants.

This was a bittersweet tradition – one that people never want to have happen but also would never miss if it had to happen. In the ten years since Evelyn and I arrived there had been a number like this, all to help those left behind from some personal tragedy. Far from being somber, these benefits were always friendly, open, and uplifting.

Townspeople milled about, some greeting friends they had not seen since the last community event. Weddings and funerals bring families together; tragedies bring communities together.

Near the rear of the stage a small table, low with ornately carved legs and covered by a checkered spread, was crowded with a dazzling array of colorful pies and cakes, lit up by carefully placed stage lights from high above.

I recognized the pair of musicians setting up on the stage – it was the bearded-one and his partner with the smiling face.

"Not so much we can say," said the beard. "Pretty much it's all been said by now." Without further explanation they launched into *The Wreck of the Edmund Fitzgerald*. Many in the crowd wept hearing that story retold, but then they moved into songs more about healing, leading with *Candle in the Wind*. Two or three songs later they pulled back, promising to do more after the auction.

Another group came on the stage, to a round of applause. This time it was all schoolkids with an enthusiastic rendition of *Stairway to Heaven*. I spotted Buster's grandson, dwarfed by a bass guitar, alongside Clarissa Carson picking away on a six-string. The lead singer hit the high notes like a natural; he was an eighth-grader I had seen bussing tables during the summer at one of the restaurants. All six performers seemed confident, like they had rehearsed for many weeks. The school's music teacher appeared just as the final notes rang out, a waif-like woman who wanted the kids out front and preferred to remain in the background.

A member of the select board stepped up to the microphone to start the auction, holding up a lofty lemon meringue pie. "You guys all know whose kitchen *this* came out of," he drawled. "Besides me, who here wants to take this pretty baby home?"

"Ten dollars," yelled out a man close to the stage.

"I hear ten dollars, do I hear fifteen?"

"Twenty," called out a woman sitting off to the side. I recognized her as Dorothy Spears, the head of the largest employer in this corner of the state.

"I hear twenty," said the auctioneer, but before he could ask for a higher amount someone else yelled out "Thirty!"

"Hey, now we're getting somewhere," he shot back. "Do I hear thirty-five?"

"Fifty," shouted the woman.

Before he could respond the first man yelled out "Sixty!"

"Seventy!" The woman looked over at the man and laughed.

The man swallowed hard and responded, "seventy-five."

With a note of triumph, the woman waved her hand and yelled out "ninety dollars!"

Evidently that was enough for him because he sat back with a grin but remained silent, gesturing to a woman seated nearby. The next one up was a big chocolate cake decorated with yellow frosting. Mrs. Spears goaded the man she'd just bested into purchasing that cake for sixty dollars.

One of the kids brought up a big white cake covered with coconut, and the auctioneer held it high. "Well, guys?"

Buster jumped up and shouted "twenty dollars."

"Oh no you don't," I heard Jake say before shouting out "forty!"

Buster looked across the room at Jake, smiled broadly and replied "sixty."

The auctioneer stood silently while the two went back and forth, with Buster finally calling it quits when Jake offered one hundred dollars. In the next exchange, Buster beat out Mrs. Spears, claiming a deep-dish apple pie for eighty-five. By the time that item was settled, Jake and his friends sat behind an empty platter showing just a few crumbs and a smear of white frosting.

I have a fondness for cherry pie, and apparently so does Dorothy Spears. Evelyn started digging in her purse when I stood up.

"Forty dollars," I called out.

"Forty-five," shouted Chester Taylor.

Before I could respond, Dorothy Spears chimed in, "sixty."

"Seventy," yelled Chester.

When I replied, "ninety-five," both sat down and one of the kids delivered the pie. While I peeled off the bills, several people seated nearby looked at it longingly, like they were hoping I was going to break out a fistful of forks and offer it up right away. "Sorry, guys," I said pulling my prize to a safe spot between Evelyn and me. Mrs. Spears probably didn't mind losing – she already had at least a half-dozen trophies lined up. Likely all would end up in her employee lunch-room the next day.

The original auctioneer stood aside while his replacement dragged the now-empty table to the front of the stage and pulled off the covering. "I think you know this here piece of furniture," he drawled. "Roger Cage made it in his shop, out'a wood his father cut from their land and let dry for three years. Heard tell it's solid maple, got eight coats o' lacquer."

A woman that I recognized as his sister joined him on stage. They both sat down on the edge of the table and he opened a bag of cookies intended for the auction. "Dorothy," he drawled while handing her one, "what do you reckon this here table ought'a go for?"

She munched down on the cookie and sat for a second or two, running her hand over the legs. "I dunno, Phil," she replied. "Sure looks nice to me."

Phil looked down at the table while chewing on one of the cookies. "Look how tight these here joints are," he said. "You c'n see 'em, can't no how feel 'em."

Dorothy reached into the bag of cookies. "Guess maybe couple hundred, for a start."

I spotted three men, leaning on different parts of the wall outside of the general crowd, pretending to not be watching closely. None had purchased pies or cakes.

"Two-fifty," called out one of the men. The crowd fell silent and parted, allowing the other two to take a step forward.

Phil turned to Dorothy. "Good cookies, no?"

"Judith Woods made them," she replied, reaching for another. "Wouldn't 'spect no less from her." A few in the crowd chuckled but all were paying close heed.

The second of the men called out "three-hundred," immediately followed by the third's "three-fifty."

"Judith made these? Really?" Phil dug into the bag and pulled out another. "I gotta get me more o'these."

"Five hundred," called the first man.

"She did," replied Dorothy, reaching into the bag. "Bet she'd make you some."

The second man went back to his spot, standing along the wall with a dejected look, but the third shouted "six hundred."

"Think she might?" Phil munched on another cookie. "I'd sure like that."

"Seven hundred," called out the first man. A few in the crowd called out encouragement but conversation had stopped.

"I 'spect she'd be willing to do that." By that time the cookie bag was empty and the crowd was all leaning towards the stage. "If you ask her real nice like."

"Eight hundred." The room fell into a pregnant silence.

"Oh, man," groused Phil. "There you go puttin' conditions on it. Knew it couldn't a'been that easy."

When the first man called out "One Thousand," the third man sat down and frowned. The first man pulled out his checkbook and the crowd burst into applause.

"We got any more of these here cookies we can sell?" asked Dorothy, polishing the table top with a soft towel apparently set aside for the purpose.

"Nah," replied Phil. "Guess you and me, we done ate them up." He accepted the check. The first man hoisted the table over his head triumphantly and carried it off with a big smile.

And so it went, with a parade of spectacular confections going out the door, or more often not making it that far. By the time the last item came up, a big platter of chocolate chip cookies, prices had dropped to the mid-thirties. Several similar platters sat empty on the tables, shared by friends among friends, enjoying fifteen-dollar brownies and the like.

It was late when the two musicians returned to the stage, and they only played a few songs while people started to pack up. The crowd that left that evening was in a somewhat better mood than when they arrived, and I suspect the pies and cakes were only a small part of it.

* * * * *

This time the news from Washington did attract some attention. The new president was calling for a bunch of budget-cuts but it seemed that few would have much effect in places that had voted for him.

The proposal to cut funding for the Coast Guard was not well received, even by Buster. "When we need 'em, they always come," he fumed. "What're they gonna do, send us the choppers from somewhere down New Jersey?" Of course, there was no answer to that. Only that the money was needed to build a wall like the one the Canadians had joked about.

"At least it's not our own Guv'ner stickin' it to us this time," grumbled Judith. "But he's not sayin' anything against it neither."

"So what kin we do?" Jake mused. "Think they gonna listen to what we say?"

"Not much we can do," Judith replied. "Our own congressional representative, he don't *never* show his face out here in Washington County." She took a sip of her drink and let out a deep sigh. "Think he's in the president's pocket. Or on his payroll."

More Thirsty Folk

The news in the big-city paper that morning had not seemed so outrageous. At least not before it was carefully read. The governor had loudly proclaimed that his new policy would save the people of Maine, as he put it, a ton of money. He would be able, thanks to recent changes in Federal education policy, to keep income and sales taxes at the same level while at the same time creating tax benefits that would surely attract important new businesses to York and Cumberland counties.

"This shows how we're working to serve the people of Maine," he thundered at a town hall meeting hastily called in Sanford to announce the action. His press secretary stepped to the podium and explained that the governor was hoping to entice General Motors to open a new assembly plant a bit south of Portland. "This will be great," bragged the governor, with the school commissioner standing behind him wearing a big smile. "Maybe a thousand new jobs."

Keisha was the only one in the bar when I ducked in to get a beer. I knew better than to accept her challenge to a round of pool, so her entreaties were in vain.

"But let me ask you," I said to her. "Did you see the paper this morning?"

"I did," she grumbled. "South of Portland? That's going to help *us* a whole bunch."

"It's worse than that," I said. "You see where he's looking to find that 'ton of money'?"

"Something about schools, right?"

"Yeah. The schools." I took a swig of beer, watching her eyes. "He wants to consolidate the school districts into county-wide and cut state funding to the bone. Apparently the new schools chief in Washington is behind this."

"What's it mean for us?"

"Simply this, we'll be paying the whole bill for our school with our property taxes, including the parts the state has mandated. And, if we don't like it, we can complain to the county."

"Complain to the county about *what*?" I turned to see who it was that had snuck in behind us. Judith Woods stood with one hand on her hip and the other waving to Annie for her regular drink. "You guys ever stop bitching about stuff?"

Keisha laughed out loud. "If what Arnie's saying is true," she said, turning to face Judith, "you're the one's gonna be *leading* the bitch parade." Judith glared up at Keisha like she didn't get the joke, then turned to me.

"Our governor's latest little trick," I snickered.

Judith picked up her drink and scowled. "Don't you guys get me started on that. We spent the last two hours upta the town office trying to figger *that* one out."

"And..." I drained my beer and signaled for a refill. "Your conclusion was?"

"Pretty damn sketchy so far. Looks like we got a nasty property tax hike coming and nothing to show for it. Chet, he's damn steamed 'bout this. So's the school supe."

"I bet *he* is."

"You know how Chet's been after that place down the county road, wants to turn it into a community center. Can kiss *that* idea goodbye. Our money's heading someplace three hunnerd friggin miles away, leavin' us high and dry."

Buster was the next to join in. I'd seen his boat coming up the narrows forty-five minutes earlier and guessed it was just about time he'd belly up to the bar. He was in a jubilant mood, and had somehow come up with a new red hat.

"You hear what the governor's doing?" he asked, ignoring Keisha but looking Judith straight on. "Told you this new guy was gonna kick butt, get things done." I'd never seen him looking so giddy.

"Uhhh..." Judith took another sip of her gin and tonic. "Buster..."

He was not to be interrupted. "This's gonna be great!" He reached for his beer and with one gulp drained half the mug. "Guy promised he was gonna make us *great* again! Can't hardly wait for that new pier go in."

"Oh?" Judith looked him with a disarming smile, maybe like the sphinx. "What've *you* been hearing?"

"Guys been talking 'bout it all day on the VHF. You din't see it?"

"No." Judith seldom had this innocent look. "I'm all ears."

"The paper this morning, big headline. Our new guy in Washington tole our governor cut some fat outa the budget and then they can get these things done. S'prised you din't see it."

"That's what you guys talk about when you're out there on the water? Any of you have that newspaper?"

"Nah." He finished draining his beer and called for another. "One o'the guys read it afore breakfast, tole us 'bout it later. *Gonna be great*, jist you wait and see." I saw the way Keisha's eyes darted back and forth between Buster and Judith, but for now she was biting her tongue.

Judith continued, staring straight at Buster. "Did they say where they was gonna cut all this fat?"

"Something 'bout the school budget," he replied. "Too much going in there anyway, plenty room to cut." Another of the fishermen came in and the two of them headed out to the deck, laughing and poking each other on the shoulder.

Keisha spoke up. "Sounds like he didn't actually *read* what was in the paper."

"I ain't gonna be the one burst his bubble," Judith chuckled. "Maybe he'll get it, maybe he won't. Somebody else's turn to be the bitch."

By the next day it was all over town. The consensus in the coffee shop was that Billy Jasper, our local state representative, would be able to muster enough support in the legislature to keep a lid on the tax hikes. When he came into town later that afternoon, he was mobbed.

"I'm sure we can get a public hearing going," Jasper said when the clamor died down a bit. "But if you guys all show up in Augusta demanding to speak they're more likely to listen."

When the tax assessor spoke up, the crowd fell silent. "From what I can see here," he said, "based on what the governor says and keeping the school funded at present levels, a property worth a hundred thousand will pay almost three hundred more each year in taxes." When he added, "at least that much," a collective groan went up. They hardly heard the last part: "Every town out here will see the same increase."

"That increase," Jasper added, "won't get us anything new. It'll only keep us where we are, just with less money to spend on other stuff."

Judith stood on the edge of the crowd, uncharacteristically silent, her black expression probably revealing more than she hoped. When she started to move to the center of the crowd, people stood aside to let her pass.

"Billy," she said. "We can fill us a school bus, maybe even two, if you can get that hearing going." She paused and looked around at the crowd. "Who here is with me on this?" All hands went up.

But of course there was to be no hearing. Downcoast legislators all supported the governor's idea, and since they had the population, they also had the votes. Portions of Billy's speech were televised but it got him nowhere, particularly since his colleague in the next district to the north-west, Larry Latham, supported everything the governor wanted with never a question. The big-city paper covered it, but ran it on page four of the second section. "Tax Revolt Fizzles," the headline trumpeted with a grinning Latham in the photograph.

I was feeling pretty bleak when I stepped into the bar that evening. Keisha and Blondie were duking it out on the pool table and Judith sat alone. She didn't even look up when I sat down next to her.

"It's cuz it's Washington County," she grumbled. "Arnie, if it's us, down Augusta they don't give two shits what happens." I sat back, nursing my beer. She wasn't done – more would be coming. The two girls finished their match and headed over towards where we sat. Blondie gave Judith a hug then the pair took seats at the bar.

"You know," she continued, "no matter how they stick it to us, somehow we'll get by. At least most of us will. And we'll do what we can for them's hurting. That's jist who we are." She took a sip of her drink and gazed out over the channel for a minute or so.

"But still, it hurts."

"So what can we do?"

I watched while she hopped down off the stool, went to the door, and stepped to the porch rail. It was a warm evening with just a light breeze, seals cavorted in the channel and birds dove for fish in the current. Two boats passed by motoring to the north, returning home with the day's catch. One was Buster's boat, *Lobster One*. Judith returned to the bar and sat back down again.

"He'd friggin' *kill* me for saying this," she said, pointing with her thumb at the red and white lobsterman grinding its way against the current. "We gotta get more going 'round here to help the tourist business. Only thing they left us we can grow."

Much as I wanted to jump in and offer my support, I held back to let her speak. Something was coming out, and I didn't want to be the one to get in her way.

Judith looked down the bar at the two girls. "Keisha..." The tall black girl looked up at her. "When're you getting done this year?"

"I got three weeks more. October first they close 'till next year."

"What will you do?"

"Don't know yet. Something'll come up." I wondered if she was as confident as her smile seemed to show. "Got my feelers out."

"And you… Doris?"

"Urchin season starts November. I'll be sternman in my uncle's boat. That and scallops'll take me to March. Unless all them boats from away force 'em close the season early."

Judith turned towards Annie, who had been lounging on the other side of her bar. She had never, as long as I'd been coming around, been much of one to speak a lot of words, or to miss them either.

"Annie," Judith asked, "If there was more people in town October, November, maybe even April… What would it mean for you?"

Annie laughed softly. "More folks in town, more thirsty folks in town." She looked across at the posters on the far wall. "More musicians getting a paycheck."

* * * * *

Chester Taylor nodded at the television cameraman, then gaveled the Select Board meeting open. Judith was there, so were the other three, and a small knot of residents sat close together near the back of the room. The board quickly dispensed with approving the minutes of the previous meeting and the other mundane tasks.

"We have a young lady who asked to speak to us this evening," Chester announced, glancing down at the next line on the

78

agenda. He looked up and spotted Tiffany Helman sitting with her mother in the fourth row. "Please," he said, pointing at the open space before the table, "come forward where we can hear you."

Tiffany stepped to the front of the room and the camera swung over towards her. I don't know if she saw her face on the monitor, but I did.

"Thank you, Mr. Taylor," she said, speaking as though she had practiced her words. She turned slightly toward the camera, but not so far that Taylor couldn't see her face.

"I know that everybody here knew my Dad, and that the whole town tried to help out that day. Mom and I know that and we're grateful for the way people came together that day and what they've done since. Daddy loved his work and was proud of being able to do it. He always said Adam Russell was a good captain kept a good boat and was good to him. Daddy and Jason Williams liked working together on Captain Russell's boat."

She paused for a second and looked back at her mother. Mary Ellen nodded in encouragement then Tiffany looked back at the camera. I watched a tear trickling down her face. The cameraman must have spotted it too because he zoomed in close, focusing on the emotions flickering across her face.

"What most people don't know was that he didn't want me to become a fisherman. He said that to me many times, insisted that I get an education so I didn't have to work on a boat, go wrinkling and dig clams in the cold, come home smelling like bait. He didn't know what I maybe could do, but was sure he didn't want me to do that. 'I want you to work with your head,' he always told me," touching her fingertip to her temple. "'Not with your back'."

A quiet sobbing was heard in the rear of the room. I glanced over my shoulder and saw Mary Ellen bent forward, clutching a handkerchief over her face. Tiffany's shoulders stiffened and the tear disappeared.

"I came here tonight because I want to ask that you do whatever is needed to keep the school as good as it is right now. Do it for all the kids, not just for me. And for my mother and her friends, that you find some way to help the town grow some business other than fishing. We all know that catch limits are getting tighter each season and the number of fish… What the DMR calls 'biomass,' that the number of fish is less and less each year."

"Tiffany," said Judith. "We all thank you for coming here to us so soon after your loss. This must be very hard for you and I know you prepared carefully before you stood up this evening. Is there something you think we should be doing to develop some other business?"

"A bunch of my mother's friends work in the restaurants and the bed and breakfast places. Anything you can do to make more people want to come here will help them. I know Mr. Taylor wants to do the community center. My mother's friends all say it would be a good thing if we did music and stuff in there, that the visitors like that and would come here to see it. We have a bunch of people around here good at music. It'd be great for them have a place to perform even in the winter. Might give some of the kids a reason to stay."

Taylor spoke up. "That's what your mother's friends say. What do *you* think would be a good thing?"

"I think the center would be a good thing too. I know there's kids sneak in there sometimes and do things that maybe aren't so good. Some day one of em's going to get hurt. Maybe also do something about the other old buildings that nobody's using, specially those that're falling down."

"Tiffany," said Judith. "Tell us about your own plans."

"I want to do what Daddy said, work with my head." She took a deep breath and glanced back. "I could have gone to work getting a lobster license going in by the student plan. I had a sponsor ready to take me on. I decided not to do that and now it's too late."

"Why's it too late?" asked another of the selectmen.

"Takes five years, student's got to finish before they hit eighteen. Start now I'd have to go the apprentice route, sit on the waiting list twenty years. Maybe more."

"So," asked Judith. "What is it you *do* want to do?"

"Go to college, learn to be a physician's assistant. That costs a lot of money and I know my Mom can't pay it. If I can get a basketball scholarship maybe I can get that done. Daddy told me he was sure I could do that and I want to try, do it for him. Then maybe I can get a job over the medical center and I can live here in my own town."

"Thank you Tiffany," said Taylor. "We appreciate hearing from you." The camera followed her to the back of the room where she collapsed into her mother's arms. After a brief pause the lensman retreated back to the front, focusing on Taylor.

"Chet," said Judith. "Tiffany's not even fifteen, nowhere near old enough to vote. But we need to listen to her now. Pretty soon she'll be the one sitting up here this side of the table, maybe trying to keep a lid on *your* taxes. Hell!" she laughed. "If she wanted, I'd even be her campaign manager."

The next day, word got around town pretty quickly that Buster Loman had confronted Judith Woods right in the middle of the street. A half-dozen people saw it, but accounts varied as to what came down. I knew he wouldn't tell it to me straight, and hoped to find Judith in a talkative mood.

"It wasn't just me," she told me that evening in the bar. "Mary Ellen Helman was with me, we was coming out of the coffee shop when he came on us. He was not happy, not one bit."

"You tole her what to say, din't you," he said in that rough voice he's got, pushing his finger at Mary Ellen. "I seen the whole thing on TV."

"You think my girl cain't think fer hersef?" Mary Ellen said right back to him. "Dun't know her very well, do ya."

"She weren't talking like no fifteen year old. You wrote them words for her. Don't say you din't."

"Buster," said Mary Ellen, as Judith later told me, "She speaks her mine, I speak my own. Whut'd she say you think is *wrong*? You ain't sed nothing lak that yet."

Mary Ellen wasn't quite done yet. According to Judith, she gave Buster a hard look before adding "You wud never speak about Tiffany lak this if her father was still here."

"I was just standing there, listening in," said Judith. "It was like he didn't even know I was there. But when she said *that*, he shut up and looked at me."

"So," I asked, "did he ever answer her question?"

"Not so much as to really say anything. Just his usual, 'Flagg's Point's always been a fishing village, ain't gonna let nobody turn it inta another friggin Bah Hahbah.' Then he turned on his heel and left, said nothing more."

"So he didn't say anything to you, only to Mary Ellen?"

"Not yet he hasn't," Judith said, lifting her empty glass to Annie for a refill. "I'm ready for him, know it's coming." She turned towards the deck where the late afternoon sun cast a deep shadow. "Not sure he's seen the next thing his favorite governor's pulled."

"Yeah," I said. "That one sounds pretty mean-spirited."

"Oh, it's all o'that. Axing General Assistance means anything we do to help someone in need, all of it comes out'a our own hide."

"I know you can't give any specifics but the town report shows you guys spent less than twenty three hundred dollars last year. Doesn't seem like so much."

"Less'n half the budget line. Bit o'that went to help a family got burned out. And a couple of our senior citizens couldn't pay for heating fuel, that kind'o stuff. The state pays us back part of what we authorize. At least they're s'posed to, long's we play by their rules."

"Why's he doing this? What do *you* think?"

"What do I think? I think that new guy in Washington makes it easy for him screw people around like that. And I don't think he's even got hisself half started."

* * * * *

The next morning when the alarm went off, Evelyn was already up on one elbow looking at me funny. "Were you *really* trying to beat me up?" she asked.

I rubbed the sleep out of my eyes and shook my head. "Don't think so," I pleaded.

"Last two hours I thought I was sleeping with one of those guys fights in a cage."

"Was I *that* bad?"

"You're asking me?" When she laughed it told me she was getting over it. She reached over and touched my face. "Did my little boy have a bad dream?"

"Now that you mention it, I kind 'a did."

She headed for the kitchen, soon returning with our first coffee of the day. "So tell Mommy all about it."

The first gulp went down quickly and the caffeine kicked in right away. "I dreamed I went to an auction."

"An auction. Okay, that's a start. Could'a gone to worse places."

"Yeah, a start. There weren't so many things there, but one was a beautiful set of teacups I thought you'd like. When they came up I opened with a fifty dollar bid."

"My hero." She continued to stare at me, now over the edge of her mug. "What'd they look like?"

"Demitasse cups, seven of them. Each was a different Chinese pattern, and each had a matching saucer."

"Seven?"

"Yeah. What he was selling wasn't quite a whole set."

"But the pattern sounds nice. I'd probably still like them." She took a sip of coffee and looked me straight on. "You didn't get them for me?"

"The auctioneer… He was a big guy with orange colored hair in a funny comb-over. And there was another guy. He wanted those teacups too but I guess he was hoping to get them on the cheap. They seemed to have some kind of a deal and when my opening bid was so high it spoiled their game."

"So what happened?"

"When the other guy asked the auctioneer if he could delay bidding until after first calling someone else, he said 'yes'."

Evelyn looked puzzled. "Calling a friend? In an auction?"

"Strange, right? He called but ended up having to leave a message. Then he asked if we could hold off just a minute or so, promised whoever it was would call back right away."

"What were they going to tell him?"

"I have no idea. Maybe that he could bid higher against me. They probably knew if I opened that high I'd go even higher."

"Did they call back?"

"Not so far they haven't."

"I never heard of an auctioneer allowing a stall like that."

"That's why it was so frustrating. The orange-haired guy was going along with whatever the other guy said, just making up rules along the way."

"What'd the other guy look like?"

"Medium height, kind of fat, scruffy hair, hadn't shaved in a week. Disagreeable looking fellow, acted like a jerk. Kept whispering in the auctioneer's ear."

"But you couldn't hear what he said?"

"No. All I saw was that the orange-haired guy was listening. That's when you woke me up."

"I like that." She rolled back and laughed. "The way you make *me* the villain."

"You ready for another cuppa?" I asked, dropping my feet to the floor.

Tiffany Speaks

Residents filed into the room, one at a time and by couples and the occasional threesome. All stopped to register – to have the Town Clerk confirm their right to vote in town business. They wandered around the room, waiting for the thump of the microphone to announce the beginning of that most New England of all traditions – the annual Town Business Meeting. As usual, it was held in the school cafeteria because it was the largest meeting room available.

The warrant contained forty-three separate articles, most of which were the routine necessaries like approving the budget line for keeping the roads open in the winter or authorizing expenditures to heat the Town Office. The school budget was passed earlier, so the opportunity to ask questions about that had passed.

Forty-eight people showed up to vote on how the Town of Flagg's Point would first raise the money, then spend the money, to continue as a town for another year. That, out of over a thousand voters who were eligible to be part of that discussion.

I scanned through the warrant, looking for anything that might be controversial. A couple items came to mind, but there was little other than the boring stuff that moved quickly.

Judith sat at the front table, facing the voters. Chester sat at the far left, closest to where the moderator would stand, and the remaining members of the Board of Selectmen took similar seats. The routine of electing the moderator took maybe five minutes, then the work began.

The first thirty-two articles took twenty-five minutes. Each one had to be read, then the floor opened for discussion. Nobody wanted to discuss the costs of garbage pickup and mowing the cemeteries was, as always, a yawner. Both were necessary and not worth a fight.

Article thirty-three asked for an increase in General Assistance, doubling the amount from the previous year. This one got some attention – several hands went up. The moderator recognized a woman from the back of the room.

"Mr. Moderator," she asked. "Can the board explain this increase?"

Chester rose and was acknowledged. "The state has withdrawn their support for this. We won't get matching funds anymore."

Judith too rose, and when Chester sat down was invited to speak. "Every year they make us update the General Assistance ordinance," she explained. "But now our governor has decided that if we have to help someone in need he's not gonna pay the state's share. Either we ask the town to have some extra money set aside now, or else have an emergency meeting when somebody's hurting."

Another voter stood and was recognized. "So what if we don't need that much?"

Judith, still standing, looked toward the moderator, waiting for the nod. "Betty," she said, "if we get lucky and there's no need, we don't spend it. It gets set aside and next year we can ask to use it for something else." The article passed by a show of hands and the meeting moved on.

Article forty-one was the one I was waiting for. It asked the town to raise funds to replace those lost by the state's withdrawal of revenue sharing, which had not been an issue as far back as anyone could recall, until now. Several people leapt to their feet, looking to be recognized by the moderator. Buster was on one side of the aisle,

Jake was on the other. I watched the moderator looking back and forth between the two, maybe trying to decide which to call on first.

Jake won the toss. "Mr. Moderator," he said, speaking loud enough to be heard in the next county. "Can you ask for an explanation where that money went?"

Judith sprang to her feet, much to Chester's dismay, and was immediately recognized. "No," she said. "We cannot. Only the governor can explain that."

Chester rose and was acknowledged. "These are funds that come from sales tax revenue. It is generated in the towns, and the state has historically shared it. Their contribution to Flagg's Point alone has dropped fifty-three thousand from four years ago to last year. That's a decline of twenty-five percent, and that's before *this* cut."

Buster was jumping up and down, waving insistently. "Yes, Mr. Loman," the moderator said as Jake sat down.

"Can't we do like they say, just tighten our belts?"

Chester scrambled back to his feet. "Sure we can." It was clear he was working hard to remain civil. "What is it you think we should give up? Maybe those new sidewalks? Or the streetlights? We can just stop doing those things. Maybe we can stop funding the ambulance service."

"Did the governor tell you to stop those?"

"No," replied Chester. "He just said we are now on our own."

By this point Jake was back up, clamoring to be recognized. "There are some of us," he said loudly, once given the floor, "that don't want to see our town just crumble into the sea. If there's no way but we take care of it ourselves, I say that's what we have to do."

Buster was not to be outshouted. "We ain't crumbled int'a the sea so far, not in more'n two hunnerd years. We gotta hold the line on these taxes some time, I say we do it now."

The argument went back and forth with neither side gaining traction and the small crowd becoming increasingly restive. I expected to see the pitchforks break out any minute, but was not sure which side would feel the pointy end. When the crowd suddenly fell silent, I turned back to see what was happening.

Tiffany Helman stood silently in the aisle, looking straight at the moderator. "Miss Helman," he began, speaking hesitantly like he was all of a sudden unsure of his position. "Only registered voters are allowed to speak."

The floor erupted with cries of "let her speak" and "at least hear what she has to say." The moderator gaveled the crowd into near-silence with one hand, fumbling through his handbook with the other.

"As moderator," he announced, holding up the book, "I am allowed to permit a non-voter to speak if I feel they have important information, or if a majority of you request it." The only hands that did not immediately shoot into the air belonged to Buster and a few of his friends. The moderator looked about the now-silent room, then back at Tiffany. "For the benefit of the clerk, please identify yourself then say what you wish to say."

"My name," she said speaking in a strong, confident voice, "is Tiffany Helman. I was born into Flagg's Point, have lived here all my life, am a student in this very school, and I intend to live my life here. To you, I am just a kid, not allowed to be part of this process. Please hear me out because this is important to me." She paused and looked around the silent room.

I followed her eyes as best I could and saw that she seemed to be seeking out those who earned their living on the water. "I believe you all know how my life changed recently." A few gasps and even sobs were heard from around the room but she stood tall and resolute.

Tiffany took a deep breath then continued. "My father wanted me to get an education and to bring my skill back to benefit the people of Flagg's Point, and I fully intend to honor his wish. But please, let this town be one that I, and others like me, will *want* to return to.

"Nobody knows where we might go if we move forward. But we all know where we will go if we *don't* move forward."

I had never seen this crowd so silent. Even Buster had nothing to say, although I was sure he would have something later on. Tiffany looked about, making eye contact with several. "Thank you for letting me speak." Then she sat down. The room remained silent, although several were openly weeping.

The moderator looked about. "Do I hear any more discussion?" Nobody spoke.

"Do you want me to read the article again?" His question was answered by a chorus of 'No!'

"Alright now, please raise your hand if you are in favor of article forty-one passing." About thirty-five hands went up. "All those opposed?" Nobody raised their hand.

The remaining two articles passed with no discussion and the meeting adjourned. Tiffany quickly left, surrounded by friends and family members.

I grabbed my jacket and headed for the parking lot. A cluster of people stood around Marilyn St. Claire, including Jake. Buster bolted from the door and headed straight for his pickup, not looking either way or speaking to anyone. A few seconds later he took off, scattering gravel with his tires. I headed over to the small group.

"Do we really have any choice?" Marilyn asked without looking up.

"You mean other than maybe just let the place go?" asked another.

"Gawd," she groaned. "My life savings is in that place."

"And mine," said Jake, "is in my boat."

"What…" said Marilyn, looking hard at Jake. "Does that mean?"

Jake took a deep breath and returned Marilyn's stare. "You all done heard what Tiffany just said. I happen to think she's right." When Marilyn made no reply, he continued. "This town is my home. I want to be proud of it. Don't you think for a minute, I can't see what's happening."

The door opened and two members of the Select Board emerged, followed a few seconds later by Judith and Chester. They spoke briefly then headed off towards their respective cars. I saw Judith looking the small group over carefully but she didn't come near, just kept walking. From her expression I was convinced she had taken attendance.

"Okay Jake," frowned Marilyn. "From what you see, what *is* happening?"

"Fisheries are tougher every year," he drawled. "Downcoast operations got all the advantages, cept'in easy access to this here bay. It's all we got, and here we got the best scallops in the world. But," he added with a pause, "scallops and clams ain't e'nuff keep us going."

"So you believe we need to start looking for something else."

"Reckon mebbe so." I started to head back to the car, where Evelyn was waiting.

The man stopped me before I could open the door. In the darkness, I recognized Harry Parker, with whom I had casually spoken several times but didn't really know.

"Arnie," he said, "got just a minute?"

"Sure," I replied. "What's up?"

"There's a few of us getting together to stage a play, and there's a role we think you'd be perfect for."

That one caught me short. "You want to put me on the stage?"

"We do." At first I thought he was kidding, but his earnest look soon persuaded me otherwise. "You'd do great playing a New York banker. Not too many lines, but a few good ones." He looked hopeful. "Ever do anything like that before?"

This time I laughed out loud. "Not since college. I forgot so many lines back then, they wouldn't let me audition again."

"Can I send you the script?"

* * * * *

A day later when I stopped in at Annie's Place for a beer, Judith cornered me. "What the hell'd you say to Marilyn St. Claire?"

"Are you asking what she said to me?"

She looked up at me with a scowl. "You know what she's got going?"

"I think you're about to tell me."

"You haven't seen her petition? It's all over the friggin' town."

When I told her I hadn't seen it, she just got more agitated. "She wants us to take on the community center project, the one got shot down four months back."

"Chet's idea?"

"Yeah. That's the one."

"Thought you were in favor of that."

"That was before our illustrious governor forced us to turn over that money for his pipe dream. We can never sell that to the voters now." She glanced up at the clock. "Hey! Gotta go." As she turned to leave, she looked back at me. "You be here a while?" I assured her I would be.

I wasn't sure what to make of all this. Flagg's Point taxes were not the lowest in the region, and they weren't the highest either. But if we were forced to surrender our dreams, then what? I, for one, was willing to pay more if it meant we got more, but I was not so

94

naive to think everybody agreed with that. There were some I knew who would be quite willing, as Jake put it, to let the town crumble into the sea.

Some parts had already done that, but mostly they were abandoned buildings like the old cat food factory down on the point. Big pieces of that went down the stream during one of the previous winter's Nor'easters, scattering debris all over our beach, littering the waterfront on the Canadian side of the channel, and giving the fishermen another headache.

While I was mulling all that over, two men came in. I know, or at least recognize, most who live in Flagg's Point – these two I didn't know. They were obviously together, spoke with a midwestern accent, and were dressed like they'd spent most of the day on the water. I guessed they had something to do with the boat tied alongside the pier; it was not a vessel like the local fishermen would use.

Twin outboards, gleaming white fiberglass with not a scratch to be seen, no radar or VHF antenna, and no fixed gear. The men were wearing expensive foul weather gear but with sneakers, and were having a great time together. Annie was more than happy to pour the expensive Scotch she so rarely got to uncork, but had a bit of trouble when one tossed down a hundred-dollar bill.

"Albert!" I heard one say to the other, "You and me, we got skunked today."

"Don't know what I'm going to tell my wife," said the other, tossing down the Scotch and gesturing for another. "I figured this bay'd be crawling with groupers."

"Hah!" roared out his companion. "You won't get nothing tonight you don't bring home something for dinner!"

"Cut the shit, Ron. You won't be getting any more'n me," grumbled the one apparently named Albert.

The pair was headed for their third round when Buster walked through the door. He had on the same foul weather gear except his was a little frayed around the edges, and he also wore big rubber boots. Annie saw him coming in and drew his usual beer.

Ron looked up from their conversation, apparently looking over Buster's sea-duds. "You," he said, "have got to be a fisherman."

Buster looked him up and down, and Albert too. I caught the way his eyes lit up when he spotted the sneakers, but otherwise his stony demeanor was unchanged. He downed half his beer, dropped one elbow on the bar, and gave the pair the kind of steely glare normally reserved for idiots like me.

"You," he rumbled, "reckon right."

"Hey, that's cool," said Albert, approaching closely. I caught the look in Annie's eye and sat back to eavesdrop.

"So are we," bragged Ron. "We're here from Ohio. That's my boat out there." Buster looked again at one then the other, but remained silent. "We read this place is crawling with groupers, but we haven't even got our first."

"That's what you read, did ye?"

"And when we got here, we saw all those other boats out there," gushed Albert. "We know you guys're on to something."

Buster chewed on a swig of beer, looking exactly like a cow working its cud. His expression was half-bemused and half-incredulous, but beyond his brief reply he remained silent. I caught the look in Annie's eye and held my peace.

"So tell us," asked Ron, "what kind of lure you use out there?"

I had never seen Buster looking like he had been caught up short. He sat clutching his empty beer mug, shaking his head. "What kind of lure?"

"Yeah. Which one does the trick? You like spinners?"

Buster's shoulders shook like he was trying not to laugh. "What kind of fisherman d'ye take me to be?"

"Hey!" said Albert. "Lemme buy you another beer. We want to know how *you* catch fish out here."

When the trio moved out onto the porch, I turned back to Annie. She was laughing.

"What?"

"Those two were in here yesterday, didn't hang around so long." I looked out at the porch. Buster was saying something, holding up one finger for emphasis, while Albert and Ron were hanging on his every word. A few minutes later Annie went out and returned with an order for a fresh round.

Buster was still holding court when Judith walked back in. When I held my finger across my lips and gestured out to the porch, she looked then turned back with a smile. "Those guys and their wives, they're staying at Marilyn's place. Hear they're spending a few bucks." A burst of laughter erupted on the porch.

"Speaking of Marilyn," Judith said, speaking quietly. "She turned in her petition today. If the signatures all pan out, she's got double what she needs to force it onto our agenda."

"So we're gonna be talking about Chet's plan again."

"Seems so." She glanced out at the porch, where Buster had his head down and the other two were leaning forward like they didn't want to miss a word. "I c'n hardly wait."

A couple of minutes later Blondie joined us, first giving Judith a big hug. She had changed out of her fishing gear but still had the tangled hair of one who had spent the day in the wind. She glanced out at Buster and the two from Ohio before turning back to the bar.

"Blondie," I asked her, "heard anything 'bout where Keisha's got herself to?" Not having seen her around town in several weeks, I was curious.

"She's gone down Ellsworth," she shrugged.

"Ellsworth! What'd she find down there?"

"Landed herself a good gig, prob'ly year round."

"Yeah?"

"Tending bar in an Irish kind'a place." She took a swig of beer. "That place's got a good business going."

"You think she'll come back here?"

"She'd love to but she says she's gotta eat. Does pretty good there." Blondie turned to watch Albert and Ron heading out the front, laughing at something Buster had said.

"See you tomorrow," Ron said to Buster with a wave. Annie picked up the pile of bills Albert dropped on the bar.

"Buster," she called out as he started for the door. "Got a second?" He was in a jovial mood and plopped down on the stool across from where she stood.

"Whassup?"

"Don't know what you said to those two…" She looked up at him, over her glasses. "But they just dropped two hundred dollars here."

"Din't say nothing," he shrugged, holding his hands out palms up. "Jist tole them a couple fishing stories."

* * * * *

The mail was waiting in the kitchen when I got home that evening, including a large envelope from Harry Parker.

"He didn't waste any time," said Evelyn. I opened the envelope and pulled out a sheaf of paper, stapled along one edge. On the cover it read "Down East Gold Rush," and the author was a woman named Dorothy Blanch. A yellow sticky-note read 'Arnie, take a look at this. We think you'd be perfect as Mr. Kinney.'

"Somebody told me they did this play once before, maybe ten years back."

"Before we got here?"

"Musta been, I don't remember it." I tossed it aside for later. "Heard tell it's based on a true story, something actually happened here, hundred years or so back."

<u>Tending Bar</u>

Who'd a figgered Buster would work out so well as a bartender? Of course, it was Annie's idea, even Buster said so. But the way visitors bellied up to the bar to hear his fishing stories while serving drinks was only a surprise to a few. His willingness to actually accept that these visitors – strangers from out of town, staying on for just a few days or so – might possibly be a good thing was what floored many of us.

"Don't be too quick sell him short," warned Jake. "He felt like he got painted in a corner after we seen what his president did and how our governor followed his lead." He leaned out over the railing, clutching his beer and watching the seals in the channel. "Knowed Buster all my life. One thing you cain't call him is 'stupid'."

Of course it didn't hurt that Albert... Remember him? He and his pal Ron were the two that first got Buster talking. They came back each day for the rest of the week they were here and wouldn't let him come up for air. Then when they went home, Albert wrote a four-page article in some big sport-fishing magazine, complete with pictures of Buster and his boat. The crowd that came after that wasn't looking for groupers. I figured that was just a ruse to get someone talking. They were hoping to find the real deal and once they found it Annie was more than happy to put it on her menu. How could anyone here have known Albert was a big-name writer?

"I was just having fun," Buster protested. "B'sides, they was buying me beers and you know how that works." The third day the pair kept him going, his wife Susan came in to see what he was talking about. I don't know if she was suspicious or what, but when she and Annie put their heads together we all figured something would happen. Yeah, go ahead, call me sexist. But I have learned to stay back when my own wife Evelyn gets together with someone like that, and Annie was no different. Can't imagine Susan Loman not playing that game too – she lived with Buster. 'Nuff said, right?

Anyway, when Buster was not out fishing, he was raking in the tips at Annie's Place. I'd stop in for a beer and see the visitors clustered around the far end of the bar. He'd be standing back pretending to polish a mug while working his way through one of his stories. Nobody ever got hurt in one of his tales, but there was enough lost ordnance left over from the war – old torpedoes and the such – that he could haul dangerous junk off the bottom for a long time. He never spoke of the *Mary Lynne* or of any of the other boats now resting on the bottom, and would likely deflect the question if asked.

The way he held his audience in thrall he could tell the same story to the same people three nights in a row and they'd all swear they'd never heard it before. Those times I was able to watch his expression, it seemed he found it funny that anyone thought his stories amusing or even tolerable.

"Did I ever tell you this one?" he asked one evening while I sat nearby. The cluster of visitors with their elbows on the bar leaned farther forward, all eagerly declaring that he had not.

"It was a hot summer morning, it was," he started, "one o'them days the moon'd bring super high water. An of course, a super high means a super low jist six hours later. One o'the guys was heading out the channel an he seen this poor thing, looked like a whale, run aground in shallow water jist out by the end o'the town beach. You know the spot?"

Most agreed they knew where he was talking about, right next to the channel.

"Anyway," he continued, "at first we thought it had'ta be a whale, right size ta'be a Minke. Guy who first seen it was on a boat could'na do nothing but he got on the VHF to an outfit nearby does whale rescues. Water was pretty high right about then, but it was fall'n fast. Poor fellow was trapped and good."

"Buster," called out one man, holding up an empty glass. He paused long enough to fill several glasses.

"Pretty soon half the town knowed what was happening. A bunch headed over ta' the flats with buckets, hop'in to keep the poor beast from drying out. One of the whale guys tole us it warn't no Minke, not a whale t'all. What it was, what they call a 'Basking Shark.' It was a young one but still way too big for even twenty people haul back to the water. Speshully," he added, standing back and gesturing, "since you could already walk all way 'round it."

He stopped talking for a few seconds and looked around the group.

"A Basking Shark, that's what it was. We could see it had gills, couldn'a been no whale. It was a shark okay, but wuzzent no dangerous one. Actually, second biggest of all fish. Jist like the biggest, the Whale Shark, it eats plankton, don't come after no people or nothin'."

He served up a few more drinks and stood back for a few seconds.

"Poor fellow jist made a wrong turn, should'a stayed out'a the channel. If he'd a' headed north o' Head Harbour, he'd still be a'baskin with his kin."

By this point it was clear Buster had the knot of visitors right where he wanted them. To a person, all eyes were on him, nobody was speaking or asking questions, and the drinks were flowing. His eyes glowed and the way he held his shoulders and the set of his jaw, he was in charge and loving every second of it. Annie watched from a distance, clearly intending to let him continue just as long as he wanted.

"So you couldn't save 'em?" asked one.

"Ever body tried hard," he replied, "but he'd 'a had to last ten, maybe 'leven hours b'fore the water'd be high enough lift 'em again. No kind'a fish kin make it that long outa water, specially in the hot sun, and he din't. Some science guys come over to study the poor beast after he died, then the next high water he got towed out to sea."

"So there's nothing left to see?"

"Nah." He paused to collect a few empty glasses, and to fill a couple more. "Was good ta' see the way ever body come together try to save 'em, but you make a wrong turn in that channel, way the current runs, won't be pretty."

Buster drew up his bulk to full height and looked down with pursed lips. "Ain't never seen this myself," he said, "but I've heard tell that sometimes, when the moon is full and the water way low, two, mebbe three big fish line up out there long'side the flats, jist lay there like they's waiting."

The visitors sat back and looked at each other, shaking their heads. One, a nervous-looking fellow wearing a sweatshirt advertising a San Francisco restaurant, put up his finger. "Buster," he asked with a bit of a quaver in his voice, "what do you think they're waiting for?"

I looked up at Annie. She was laughing but put her finger across her lips. Judith came in and took the seat next to me, but stayed quiet giving him time to answer.

Buster continued. "If I was a bettin' man," he said with a drawn-out Downeast drawl, "they's hoping to see the Second Coming o' the Big Fish."

"There you have it, Bert," laughed another of the visitors, slapping the nervous-looking man on the back. "Better get down there tonight, check it out!" The group surged forward, clamoring to have empty glasses refilled.

"You'd think he'd done this all his life," Judith muttered. "Never before had any time for people didn't live here forever." I looked at her but she was looking over at Annie, wearing an expression that said she was not particularly interested in Buster's story.

"What do you think," I asked her. "Maybe he's starting to see things different now?"

"We're gonna find *that* out real soon," she replied, working on her gin and tonic.

"Don't tell me, let me guess. Marilyn's petition is on the agenda?"

"You are *so* smart," she grumbled.

* * * * *

The news got around town very quickly, how one of the visitors had wrecked his stern-drive trying to get to what looked like a beach. Buster, as the new ambassador to the fishing-tourists was early to the conversation.

"That's where the ferry dock used 'ta be," he told a group later that day. The crowd had gathered around the trailered boat, gawking at the mangled propeller and leaking oil.

"Ferry dock?"

"It was a big dock for side paddle steamers, built over hunnerd years ago. Them concrete pilings with the re-bar stickin' up is all that's left. That, and Ferry Street."

"Guy thought it looked like a nice place for a picnic," observed one, "he had no idea why nobody was using it."

"Hey," said Buster. "He got off easy. Water down six inches, he'd 'a tore the bottom out of his boat. Down a foot, he'd 'a seen that stuff. Round here, we all know 'ta stay clear o' that spot."

* * * * *

Townspeople started filing into the Town Office meeting room, gradually filling it. A few ducked into the adjacent fire hall and dragged back more folding chairs, but there was little space left for them. Chester stood at the front, with Judith seated on one side and Tiffany on the other. A quick count showed better than fifty people, including Buster and many of his friends. I also spotted Keisha in the crowd, sitting near the rear like she hoped not to be noticed. Marilyn St. Claire sat in the center of the front row, clutching a folder full of papers. Blondie sat in the rear, next to Keisha, with Mary Ellen Helman on her other side.

Evelyn had told me she wanted to go, but had a gallery opening down in New Hampshire that she had already committed to, so this evening I was on my own.

Chester harrumphed the meeting to order. "This is a Public Hearing," he announced. "But just because we won't have a moderator doesn't mean we don't expect people to be civil. There won't be any votes tonight, no decisions made." He looked around the room, making eye contact with many. "We are only here to

105

discuss this idea and listen to suggestions." The people remained silent but there was a bit of noise from seats being moved around.

He pointed at the easel with the poster-sized spreadsheets and large photographs. "We went through this during the last hearing, few months ago. Does anyone want to go over the details again?"

One voice was heard. "Anything changed?"

"Nothing." He looked around the crowded room. "I have asked Marilyn St. Claire to tell us what the people who signed her petition told her."

Chester sat down and Marilyn rose. "Thank you Chester. I took the liberty of asking Tiffany Helman to help me with this." The teenager rose and stood next to Marilyn.

"Many of us in this community are invested in serving visitors, in the hospitality businesses, the restaurants, the gift shops, and even the grocery store and gas station. Together we provide seasonal employment to over a hundred of our neighbors and full time to several dozen. They tell us if there were some way we could make the season longer their employees would have an easier time making it through the winter."

She held up several long sheets of paper filled with signatures. "We have heard from nearly two hundred Flagg's Point voters. They all want to revisit the idea Mr. Taylor floated earlier this year, to have a chance to maybe make it a better idea. His suggestion, a community center with a home for music and theatre, we think would help year round and give us more reason to promote Flagg's Point for visitors.

"Tiffany," she said, turning towards the teenager. "Please tell the people here what it was you told me the other day."

The teenager took a deep breath and began. "There's a lot of us around here that are good at making music. Maybe that doesn't include me, but we all know who they are. Annie is great at giving bands a place to perform but her place can only hold so many. Also many of us have acted in one of the plays but we can't always use the school specially in the summer when maybe we could get the visitors in."

"What she's not telling you," interjected Marilyn, "is that this would be just one more reason why somebody like her might want to return to Flagg's Point after college."

Chester stood back up and looked around the room. "Here's my suggestion," he said. "I think we should form up a committee, look into this, come back in a month." Several voices spoke in agreement.

Judith rose. "I'll be on that committee," she said, looking around the room. "Buster!" she called out. "Can we count on you to be part of this too?"

If he answered I didn't hear it over those expressing their own opinions of his involvement. Judith simply smiled but said no more.

"Judith," said Chester. "You should chair this group until you get together and pick your own."

"You all know how to reach me." Judith looked around the room. "We need your help."

With that, Chester concluded the meeting and people started following Buster out the door. A noisy cluster gathered around Judith, who busily wrote down names and phone numbers.

I caught up with Keisha in the parking lot. "Whassamatter," I said to her. "No decent pool tables in Ellsworth?"

She looked back and laughed. "Hi, Arnie. No," she said. "At least none as friendly as Annie's."

"So," I asked her, "what do you think of this?"

"Nobody's asking me to pay for it," she shrugged.

"Okay… Does that mean you don't think it's a good idea?"

She turned to face me. By this point the lot was nearly empty, except for the few remaining inside with Judith. "Listen," she said. "I'd rather live in Flagg's Point than anywhere else. But I do like eating regular-like, paying my bills too. If this idea flies and I can work a couple months more each year, I'll move back in a heartbeat."

"Yeah," I replied. "I hear the 'but'."

"Alright." Keisha laughed. "Now, about that pool table."

By the time we got down to Annie's Place, Buster had attracted a crowd but the table was open. I chalked up a stick while she racked the balls.

* * * * *

The next evening when I finished telling Evelyn how Keisha wiped my sorry butt all over that pool table she was doubled over, laughing hysterically.

"What" she gasped out, "did you think was going to happen?"

108

"I knew I wasn't about to beat her," I groused. "But she cleared the table three times before I got my first shot. Wouldn't you know, I blew that one."

"Sounds like you blew it all."

"Let me tell you what she did to me." Evelyn sat back with that bemused expression that always set me off. "At one point, she was playing the solid balls and only had one left on the table but it was blocked by all of mine. She didn't say anything, just set up her shot. It went through two of mine, then hers dropped, just as nice as could be. All she said was, 'rack 'em up'."

"How much did you lose?"

"Just the cost of a drink." I went on to tell her how, after I threw in the towel, Keisha ended up in the group of fishermen clustered around Buster. Last I saw she was at a corner table deep in conversation with one of the younger men – one that I knew she had dated, a fellow her age. I didn't stick around to hear Buster's conversation, instead ducked across the street to find dinner. Since I was a bachelor until the next day, dining out was part of the deal.

Evelyn knew that I often spoke with Jack, the owner of the restaurant, and that he knew how to tell when she was out of town. Most of the year he called Georgia home and stayed in Flagg's Point only those months he could keep his doors open. He saw me coming in and had the wine list on the bar before I sat down.

"So what's the buzz?" He pulled the cork on a nice Malbec. "They decide anything at that big pow-wow?"

"Only to set up another committee."

"Isn't that what they always do?"

"Pretty much, yeah." I turned to look out over the harbor, letting my eyes follow the silvery moonlit path across the bay to Eastport, five or six miles by water but most of an hour's drive away. "Sometimes something comes of it. We can only hope." He took off to serve a couple I knew, lived out on one of the town's more remote back roads. They sat at a table, which I took to mean they really didn't want to talk.

A few minutes later he was back in front of me, wiping down the bar top. "Jack," I said. "You're closing in a week, right?" I looked about the place – the other couple and I, we were the only ones in the place, other than the owner and four employees. He replied in the affirmative.

I knew that he provided employment, mostly part-time but with two full-timers, to about a dozen. "What would it take," I asked him, "for you to stay open another month?"

He leaned over the bar and dropped his voice down. "Arnie," he said, "I absolutely detest closing. I hate what it does to some really good people. For me to keep them on for another month?" The insistent ringing of the phone interrupted his thoughts but a minute later he was back.

"This time of year all I want is to come close to breaking even. I make good enough money in July, August, when the summer crowd's in. November's not usually so bad heat wise, I don't have to make all that much. After that it'd all go up the chimney just to have my staff standing around."

He took a deep breath, glanced around at the empty tables, and continued. "If Marilyn St. Claire can fill half her beds, enough of them come here I can keep a few of my guys on. Otherwise..." About that time a party of four came in and he got busy.

"There you go, there's your benchmark." Evelyn sat back on the porch the following evening, took another sip of wine, and looked out across the field. A thunderstorm was brewing and the sky was rapidly darkening, distant rumbles punctuated the silence. "What's that, three, four couples in town beyond the full-timers?"

"Doesn't sound like much." I refilled our glasses and sat back. "But how to make that happen?"

"What about Taylor's idea?"

"There's some in town think it's the ticket. I'm willing to give it a go. We can afford the taxes. If it keeps our people working we'll end up paying less, long run."

"You going to join that committee?"

I tipped the chair back and put my feet up on the porch rail. "Maybe."

She gave me one of those looks that always meant more than she hoped. "This stuff is getting to you," she said after what seemed a long time.

"Am I that obvious?"

"My love," she replied, "after all these years, don'cha think maybe I can figure out when something's up?"

Of course she had me on that point. Maybe I could hide my thoughts from most, but not from Evelyn.

"My whole life has been on the move," I said, sipping my wine. "From following my father around the country and sometimes beyond, to chasing that rainbow as an adult, crossing from one coast to the other and back. I've always been an outsider, just didn't know it."

She didn't say anything, just continued that look.

"This is the first time in my whole life I feel like I've become part of the community."

She reached across and squeezed my knee. "I know."

Off in the distance, to the west, we both heard the commotion. Coming from down the road, the noise started gradually but built rapidly. Sirens and the honking of many horns preceded the caravan, but then it hove into view. One of the town's fire trucks led with lights flashing and siren hooting and a blaring horn, with a school bus immediately behind, followed by at least twenty cars, all with horns blowing. They passed by slowly but making as much noise as possible, escorting the bus the last ten miles into town.

"Our kids must have won the tournament," Evelyn observed. "Half the town was in Bangor the last three days."

"I heard Tiffany Helman was one of the top scorers."

"When I was in school," Evelyn mused, "basketball was never a big deal. Out here…"

I followed her over to the edge of the porch to watch the parade disappear down the road. "Yeah. Biggest thing around. And this might be the best news we'll hear."

* * * * *

This storm was a bit more than the weather service called for, at least early on. The forecaster out on Nova Scotia – the slightly wacky one – he was the one that predicted this was coming four days before it hit.

112

But now, after three days, it had started to get to folks. You could tell by the way they'd duck into the hardware store or the grocery, jacket pulled tight and head down, forgetting about the usual cheery greeting. When the wind takes people's breath away, they get edgy.

A Nor'easter can do that, with the gusts often topping sixty and occasionally a lot more, bringing trees down and worse. Six inches of rain over forty-eight hours didn't make it any easier, but at least it wasn't cold. Last time it blew like this, the big church on the hill lost a century-old stained glass window, scattering bits of pieces of colored glass over several pews but fortunately not threatening the huge organ.

On my way over to the waterfront I spotted Jake coming out of the hardware store and invited him into my car and out of the downpour. A good crowd had gathered in the wharf parking lot, watching the chaotic waters and the boats struggling in the four and five foot waves. When the wind howls down the St. Croix River and the Western Passage, Eastport provides little shelter and the twenty mile fetch means the seas rise tall. Even Dudley Island provides scant defense when the northern winds are blowing.

But the wind-driven waves are only part of the story.

With the usual twenty-foot tides, the current flow is both predictable and inexorable. When a four-knot current flows at an angle to the wind, the boats are forced to face the seas broadside, wallowing dangerously as each trough is followed by a windblown crest shouldering its way into the shallower waters. A lobsterman, lacking the top-hamper of a dragger, has a better chance but only marginally. A boat that faces danger head-on can stand up to nearly anything – not so when it stands sideways or stern-to. When this happens during winter conditions, ice build-up has sunk more than one vessel, going down right at its mooring.

This morning there would be no ice, but there were several fishermen prepared to put skiffs in the water if their boat looked like it was in danger of foundering. "Guys have died trying that," Jake muttered as we watched out of the car window. It didn't look like any of the men on the wharf were about to defy the storm, but desperation makes for tough decisions. Every fisherman is a gambler.

Jake's boat, *Three Nine's Fine*, was riding okay, and a little closer in Buster's *Lobster One* appeared to be holding its own. Maybe that was just the luck of the draw, plus they were both still rigged for pulling lobster traps, and unburdened.

A hard gust rocked the car, shaking us like we would be blown against the hillside behind the wharf parking area, and a torrent of rain partially obscured our vision. Out in front, *Rogue Wave*, a forty-two foot dragger loaded down with an urchin dredge and a tall rig took a wave over the starboard rail, momentarily swamping the deck. It wallowed and staggered and the blast rolled it hard onto the port side beam ends, reducing the freeboard to zero.

I held my breath for a near-eternity before the antenna began to climb back towards the sky and a waterfall gushed out of the scuppers. When it finally lurched back to near-vertical, she rode noticeably lower and a half-inch stream of water appeared, flowing out of a fitting on the port side.

"Shit!" Jake muttered. "Bill Andrews' boat. He done got his cabin flooded. Musta stove in the companionway boards." He shook his head. "Pumps gonna take forever ta' clear that." Several men rushed to the point on the shore closest to the stricken boat and stood, gesticulating against the howling wind. *Rogue Wave* was now riding bow down, tugging hard against the rode like it wanted to rip the mooring out of the bottom. "He's with his wife in Bangor. She's in the hospital." He stared out of the windshield. "That's why he didn't pull that friggin' dredge off," he grumbled as if talking to himself. The stream of water pumping out of the side looked puny in the gale, like a crewman pissing against the tide.

Another large wave bore down on the boat, this time crashing over the bow. A foot of green water swept across the wheelhouse roof and poured onto the deck, but this time the scuppers kept up, at least mostly.

Buster drove onto the wharf, towing a skiff. "He's not going out there," I blurted out in horror. "Is he?"

"Not without me, he ain't." Jake put his shoulder against the wind to shove the car door open and dashed across the parking lot, head down. Several men helped the two wrestle a pump out of the back of Buster's truck into the skiff, then he backed the trailer down the kelp-strewn ramp. When he jumped out another took his place behind the wheel.

The skiff was floated off with Jake holding the pump and Buster lowering the outboard into place while the truck raced back up the ramp, leaving them to confront the tempest alone. By this time I was on the edge of the parking lot, standing with a small crowd.

Within a long couple of minutes the skiff was dancing alongside *Rogue Wave*. Jake clambered on board then leaned over the side to grab ahold of the pump, seemingly ignoring the wildly pitching deck that threatened to hurl him overboard with every lurch.

A chain swung drunkenly, hanging down from the rig, but he paid it no heed. The skiff tipped up on one side like a sudden gust would flip it but Buster continued to hoist the pump up and over the rail, pushing while Jake pulled, then dragged himself on board. As soon as his weight was off the skiff, a gust picked it up and it slid under a wave.

A minute later a large hose was hanging over the starboard side, next to the wheel. We stood helplessly watching while stinging sheets of rain slanted across the wharf and the waves crashed against the rip-rap, sending salt spray into the howling winds. It was not possible to stay dry and none of us tried.

We all cheered when the four-inch stream started flowing fast and heavy, but at this point the skiff was flooded. Obviously the pump had been started without incident, but the sound was carried off by the wind. When Jake waved, we barely made out he was holding a microphone. One of the men on the shore dove into his pickup and grabbed a hand-held.

"Hey Cap'n," the man next to me said into the radio. "You fellers hav'n fun out there?"

"Jist hunky-dory." Jake's voice was scratchy and the wind got into the mike and the pump engine droned loudly, but he was still clearly audible. "Got 'nuff stuff out here, we're fix'n this busted board," he radioed back. "But maybe we gonna need us a lift."

The only thing still visible of Buster's skiff was the top of the outboard and while the storm raged there was little hope of getting it refloated and the engine started. Two men backed a truck with another skiff to the top of the ramp.

"All set," the man radioed back. "You jist say when." By this time *Rogue Wave* was riding noticeably higher in the bow and not pulling quite as hard.

A man I had spoken with occasionally at Annie's said to me, "Them guys out there, they us'ta be partners." He pointed at *Lobster One*.

"Partners?" Nobody'd mentioned this story to me, at least not before now. "What happened?"

The man shrugged. "Buster done bought him out." He turned back towards the bay where gobs of frothy foam continued to blow off the wave tops.

Jake's voice crackled over the radio again. "Bill's got hisself a cribbage board out here. Buster and me, we gonna play us a match."

The reply was immediate. "We be ready with yer ride when you need it, Cap'n."

"Hey," Jake radioed back. "How long ta' high water?"

"N'uther hour."

"So this friggin current's gonna change right soon."

"Already started to."

"You see Bill Andrews…" Jake's voice crackled across the airwaves. "You tell him he owes us a beer."

* * * * *

Two weeks after the big storm rehearsals began on *The Down East Gold Rush*. Harry Parker was the only one who knew beforehand who would be taking on which roles and I, for one, looked forward to learning who I would be sharing the stage with.

Of course, knowing who would steal the show wouldn't come until we heard the audience's reaction, which would come much later. Parker had made arrangements to use the stage in the school cafeteria, with profits going to a local charity.

The play told of a real episode in the town's history, dramatized more recently by one of the town's leading literary lights. Dorothy Blanch described how in 1898, Rev. Prescott Ford Jernegan

– a Baptist minister from Martha's Vineyard – convinced investors and townspeople alike that he had a process that extracted gold from ordinary seawater.

Furthermore, because of Flagg's Point's twenty foot tides, it was the perfect place to collect this untold wealth. Even better, it required local labor to build thousands of 'accumulators' and the infrastructure to support them. Lots of labor, and nice paychecks to go with those jobs. The outfit was duly incorporated as the "Electrolytic Marine Salts Company" and began attracting investors and others.

According to the Reverend Jernegan these gadgets operated by using mercury and an electric current, together with a 'secret ingredient,' to extract gold that he and his shadowy partner Mr. Fisher claimed was dissolved in sea water. Of course, as a man of the cloth, his word was not to be challenged.

I was slated to become a wealthy New York banker named Kinney – an investor wooed by Jernegan for his wealth and also by a genuine Gold Digger named Diamond Lil, played by a local woman a bit younger than me.

Tiffany Helman landed the role of Pauli'Nee, a town-girl who worked at the big hotel – the Ne-mat-ta-no – where Jernegan and his team took lodging, and where moneyed visitors like me, and those claiming to be, were also put up.

It was clear from her lines in the opening scene that Pauli'Nee was one of the few skeptics, terming Jernegan "a nut," but she was in the minority. Besides, who would take business advice from a teen-aged chambermaid?

* * * * *

"Heard tell you fellas're gonna do Klondike over again." Judith sniffed at her gin and tonic. "Story of a swindle."

"Sounds like fun to me."

"I'm sure it will be." She sipped at her drink and let out a deep sigh. "Folks today see it as a big joke."

"Sounds like you don't."

"My grandfather din't see it like that. Jernegan and Fisher, them bastards stiffed his fam'ly. Din't pay for a bunch 'a lumber, left 'em to cover the payroll. Jist run off in the night. Hurt a bunch 'o people 'round here." She took a sip and a deep breath. "Took some a while get over it."

"So maybe there's a lesson needs to be retold."

"'Spect mebbe so." She turned and looked out at the channel, apparently attracted by the sound of a diesel engine laboring against the current, where *Lobster One* was making its way back toward the commercial pier laden with catch and big blue bait-bins, followed by *Rogue Wave*.

For now, we were the only patrons in Annie's Place, although others would probably be coming in soon enough. I watched her eyes, she was following the second boat, now rigged for lobster.

"I know you was out there watching when Jake and Buster pumped out Bill Andrews' boat, kept it from sinkin' in the storm." I told her I had found the whole thing to be quite admirable, the way they just took it on themselves to do the right thing.

"Grew up with them two guys. Was in the same class all the way through school. No s'prise for them t'a do that. It's jist who they are."

"I knew you'd known them a long time."

"Back them days, they was always together, thicker'n thieves, them two." She took a sip of her drink and laughed. "Can't say how many times they got hauled in'ta the principal's office together. But when they got old enough to work a boat, ever body wanted 'em 'cuz they worked so hard. Both of 'em, got their lobster licenses a'fore they graduated."

"They went the student route?"

"Yeah. Kind'a sad Tiffany Helman d'int do that too. She could end up on the apprentice wait'n list twenty years, mebbe more."

"Sounds like it was her choice not to go into fishing."

"So she says." Judith turned back towards the channel. "*Lobster One*, that boat b'longed to both of 'em when they got started. Partners, they were. Borrowed the money, paid it off ahead of what they agreed."

"So now it's Buster's boat."

"Neither of 'em never tole nobody what happened that day." She gestured to Annie for a refill. "Ever body in town cud see the shiner Jake brung home. Buster looked like he done got thrashed. Two days later Buster paid off Jake's half and then he went and bought *Three Nines Fine*, been runnin' it ever since. Both of 'em, they keep good boats. Ever fisherman in town'd work the stern for either of 'em."

She turned and looked out at the channel again. The Mulholland Light, over on the Campobello shore, slowly blinked into the gathering dusk. "So... When're you guys putting on the show?"

"First weekend in December," I told her. "Three performances. You coming?"

"You'll see me at all three."

* * * * *

Rehearsals continued, with each of us struggling to master our roles. Dorothy Blanch had done a bang-up job, the rainbow of personalities that make up a town were all there. Not only do I, the money-bags banker from away, fall prey to the blandishments of Jernegan, I also find myself the target of a bona fide Gold Digger, a shady character named "Diamond Lil," played by a woman who very fortunately got along well with Evelyn.

At one point Lil contrived to intercept Kinney in the woods, pretending to be searching for berries while he took his daily constitutional.

DIAMOND LIL   Mr. Kinney, would you think me presumptuous if I asked you to join me for a little drinkie in my room before supper?

KINNEY   You mean you have spirits in your room?

DIAMOND LIL   You bet your bottom dollar! I smuggled it in. Ain't I a devil? I'll smuggle you in too and we'll have that little drinkie and maybe I'll get to know your first name.

The manager at the Ne-ma-ta-no, played by an indomitable woman from a neighboring town, was furious when learning that Lil

– a single woman – had brought "a man" into her bedroom. Her ire was expressed both in words and a chilling stare that left no doubt of her disapproval. But Lil had played the subtext to a fine point and every adult in the audience knew what she was offering.

"Sounds like you're being set up as a patsy," Evelyn told me the next evening as we sipped wine on the front porch.

"I think it's fun," I replied. "Not every day I have women fight over me."

"My poor baby," she scoffed. "Are you feeling a wee bit neglected?"

"Wait'll you see how they fight over *him*."

"But he's a preacher-man, right?"

"So he says." I took a sip of wine. "Pauli'Nee's not buying any of it."

"Who?"

"Tiffany Helman's character."

"I knew there was a reason I like that girl."

"But the story itself…" I drew a deep breath and looked off into the sunset. "Somehow, it's all too familiar."

"False promises?"

"Yeah. Promises that people want to believe in, but fundamentally are nothing more than deception."

"People are gullible?"

"I have no sympathy for the rich investors. They're sophisticated, should know better. It's the little guy that gets hurt, the one who maybe can't see through it, gets taken advantage of because he's hoping for something better, doesn't know it's a chimera."

The Gold Rush

This time when the townspeople came crowding into the school cafeteria I sat at one of two tables at the front, facing the audience. Marilyn St. Claire sat in the center seat, and Judith sat at the other table, with the other elected officials. Tiffany Helman sat at the committee table, next to Marilyn. The ad-hoc committee had held four meetings, all open to the public, and was now prepared to talk.

"I remind you again," rumbled Chester, "that this is a Public Hearing. We won't be voting but we do ask that you remain civil."

Looking around the room, there were maybe sixty people. Buster and his friends sat over on the left, in his accustomed spot. Jake sat quietly with his wife Marlene, on the right near the rear. Evelyn had found a seat near the rear, right in the middle.

"Marilyn," Chester continued. "Perhaps you can begin this by telling us what has been added to the proposed plan since we last met."

"Thank you Chet," she said, striding to the center of the room. "To start with, we have had the county plumbing inspector evaluating the old car wash and laundromat facilities. They tell us that these can be renovated and put back to work but with some investment needed. We are recommending that the town lease these to people who wish to make that investment then run them as a business, either separately or together. In other words, give someone the opportunity to start up a business that provides the town with something we all know we need."

A few people on the right applauded and Buster craned his neck to see who they were.

"As far as creating a theatrical venue in the old shop… We have a group here in Flagg's Point who are eager to get going with that, and another group from across the bridge. They promised they would work to make sure the stage was properly designed and would help pay for it. A musical instructor from Machias is on board to help make sure it also works for bands and small orchestras."

A few more people applauded but Buster sat stony-faced looking straight ahead.

"The Women's Club wants to help with furnishing and decorating the Community Center, and the Masons have volunteered to fix up the old kitchen. Two of our churches say they want to rent that space for special events."

Jake rose and waited for Marilyn to acknowledge him. "Do you have a cost estimate for all this?" Buster sat back with his arms clenched across his chest, his face darkened into a scowl.

"Chester's original estimate was quite close." Marilyn pulled the cover off a large spreadsheet and started pointing out the numbers. "Our best calculations show a total, including all we've spoken of plus a new roof, of just under three twenty-five. Factoring in lost tax revenue, it comes down to an annual tax increase of about fourteen dollars and twenty five cents per hundred thou assessed value. This assumes a thirty year state bond and we put fifty thou down." She turned back to the crowd. "We might even be able to get a grant to cover part of it."

This was apparently as much as Buster was ready to hear. He leapt to his feet, his glowering eyes darting between Marilyn and Chester.

"How," he demanded, shoving his finger in their direction, "is this going to help the fishermen?"

Judith rose to respond. "Buster," she said, "I'm real glad you asked that question." She met his glare with a demure smile. "Annie tells me you have been great for her business, bringing in a lot from our visitors. And..." She raised one finger, as if to make a point, "she tells me, you have been doing quite well yourself with tips."

"What's all that got to do with this here?" he shouted from the rear, pointing at the big spreadsheet.

"Who d'ya think is bringing that money to town?"

"Those guys come here to fish!" His voice had taken on a tinge of desperation.

"I'm sure they do," replied Judith, dropping her voice down. "You think that's the *only* reason they come here? I don't see none of their *wives* heading out on them boats. They sit in the coffee shop or make the circuit, hitting all the gift shops, checking out the library and the beach."

I spotted Susan Loman reach up to drag Buster back into his seat. She whispered something to him and he sat back with his lips clenched.

Blondie was the next to rise. She looked around the room then back at Judith, who had remained standing. "If you guys're telling us these numbers are the right ones, count on me to vote we do it."

"That's good to hear," Judith replied. "Can you tell us why?"

"Yes I can." She looked around the room again, mostly at the people who were parents of young children. "My daughter Clarissa. Over to the school they tell me she's got music in her. I want to make sure there's a place she can call home if that's what she wants to do. Same goes for the rest of the kids in this town. Right now, 'ceptin the school, they got nothing."

I leaned over towards Tiffany. "You told us something the other day. Remember what it was?"

When she nodded and rose, Judith looked over. "Another of our committee wishes to speak."

"Like I said before, I want to be proud of my town," she said in a loud and clear voice. "I want visitors to see nice things when they drive into Flagg's Point. I want them to think they have come to the right place." Looking around the room, her eyes lit up when she spotted her mother sitting next to Bethany Williams, the widow of her father's shipmate. "When I bring my friends home with me from college, I want them to know I'm part of a beautiful town."

When Tiffany sat down Chester again rose. "Anything more?" When nobody else rose, he continued. "I want to thank everyone for coming out this evening. We'll be calling a Special Public Meeting to vote on this in three weeks. Watch for the posting and the warrant." Evelyn joined me and we left together. Several groups clustered in the parking lot, but this time Buster stood alone.

Later that evening I sat with Evelyn on our porch, enjoying each other's company, a glass of wine, and the glorious Flagg's Point sunset.

"What," she asked, "do you think is going to happen?"

"Probably Buster'll fire up his damn phone tree again. I know what I hope, I also know what I fear. I don't have good feelings about this."

Evelyn gave me one of those looks that said she was waiting for me to say more.

"Some of the town's good people seem to think if we do something different we keep the past from coming back."

"So how'd we get to this point?"

"I've been asking myself the same question." I reached over to touch the back of her hand. "Don't have a good answer."

"Is this just a minor act in a bigger drama?"

Mulling her words over, I fell silent for a few moments. "Maybe I'm just too close to things to understand what you mean."

Evelyn rose, stepped to the porch rail, and turned to face me. "The pendulum," she said, "has swung way off to the right. A darkness has settled over much of our land."

"How very poetic." I took a sip of wine and looked up at my wife of many years. "You think it'll swing back again?"

"Always has."

I thought about that for a minute. "What do you suggest *we* can do?"

"Something'll come up." She sat back down next to me. "You just keep your eyes open."

* * * * *

I never saw Judith looking so glum before, but this time she looked like the world had come to an end. When I slid into the seat next to her she glanced up.

"Arnie," she said, "we lost another one."

"Another one?"

"Guess we did keep it kind'a quiet. A big outfit, fish packing with a restaurant, was looking to come here. They pulled out, gave us the word just today."

I flagged down Annie for a beer, then turned back to Judith. "Go on."

"We been talking to them on the q-t for maybe three, four months. They wanted a place to build new, start with six new full time jobs, then maybe add a bunch more. Had a spot in mind down Front Street where they could snag the tourist trade. I seen their plans, looked real nice."

"So what happened?"

"Beals Island, that's where they're going."

"What made them give up on us?"

"They got wind that we don't have any ordinances take care of decrepit buildings, were afraid they'd put up a new place but then have a neighbor let their place go and they'd lose out. Said nobody'd come to them if they was surrounded by some of the places we got right now. 'Too much risk,' they said."

"So they went elsewhere 'cuz we don't have that Dangerous Building Ordinance Chet wanted?"

"That's what they told us. Seems other places kin take care of things we can't get done."

* * * * *

It was maybe three days later when Blondie tracked me down at Annie's Place. "Arnie," she said, "about the laundromat and car wash…"

"Yeah?"

"They still available?"

"Far's I know," I told her. "But nobody can do anything until the town votes. That's in two weeks or so."

"Then what?"

"If the town goes for this, then the next step's up to the Select Board. They'll have to put that part out to bid. See what someone is willing to lease it for."

She turned away, sipping on her drink. If she said anything more, I don't remember it. But I do remember the hungry look in her eyes.

There was a lot of talk during those few weeks. Mostly I tried to lay low, figuring my task had been completed. It was all up to the town now. Way I saw it, we could either push ourselves forward, or we would slide backwards – there'd be no standing still. As usual, Buster and his crowd was the wild card.

"This thing's got you down," Evelyn said to me a couple weeks after the meeting.

"Guess it must show." I knew full well there was nothing I could hide from her.

"Not like you to be avoiding this kind'da thing." I didn't want to admit she was right, but I couldn't deny it either. To me, this was the dilemma: Could the town ever truly agree on anything? Or was it fated that we'd be forever factionalized, surrendering the town's destiny to those with the loudest voices? It has often been remarked that democracy can be messy, and right about now there didn't appear to be anyone with that big mop and bucket.

But dammit all, there was no way I could avoid the entire drama. After all, Flagg's Point was my town too and I very much wanted to be part of it. The Tuesday evening before next week's big vote Evelyn insisted we go to Annie's Place, particularly since she'd heard the music would be provided by the same duo as we'd enjoyed so many times – the guitar player with the lumberjack beard and his musical partner with the smiling face. She didn't say it but I was sure her real goal was getting me out of the house, maybe stop moping.

We took one of the small tables back near the door to the deck, hoping maybe to enjoy the music but duck out of the discussions. The pair had already begun before we arrived, and we wove our way through the crowd just as they started a new piece.

Well I'm not braggin' babe so don't put me down
But I've got the fastest set of wheels in town

When the crowd responded with

You don't know what I got!

it was very clear who owned the floor.

Evelyn leaned over so I could hear what she had to say. "You hardly expected anything else, did'ja?"

"Not really," I confessed. If I wanted to tell my wife something, there were plenty of opportunities elsewhere. Besides, if we wanted we could escape the chaos by retreating to the deck. Looking around, I spotted Judith with her elbows on the bar, listening intently to something Blondie was telling her. Neither seemed to notice the mayhem behind them, out on the floor.

The band continued from one song to the next, jumping from the hits of one decade to another. It was like Annie'd hired them to keep people dancing and not talking. I was more intent on admiring the glow in Evelyn's eyes than in paying attention to the going's on.

Maybe that was why I missed it when Blondie took off, but when Judith pulled up a chair and sat down at our table I knew something was afoot. "We gotta talk," she said. I had the distinct impression she meant both of us.

"What'd you say to Doris Carson?" she asked. Evelyn glanced at me but I was confused.

"I don't know," I replied. "Don't remember saying anything."

"You know she's itching to take over the laundry and car wash in that building you guys want us to buy. Right?"

"No," I replied, trying to be heard over the music but not beyond the table. "She asked me about it, never said she wanted it."

Judith rolled her eyes and sighed. "How is it guys can be so freakin' dense?" she grumbled, looking over at Evelyn. "Is he always like this?"

"Pretty much," Evelyn laughed. "Lately, at least most of the time." She put her hand on my arm and squeezed.

Judith pressed on. "So when Blondie put that question to you, what'd you tell her?"

"That you guys would have to put it up for bid. And that would only happen if the town went along with buying the place." I shrugged. "That was all."

"And you didn't bother asking her why she was asking them questions?"

"Didn't think anything of it."

"Okay." Judith took a deep breath and leaned forward on the tiny table. "Here's the deal. She wants it so bad it makes her teeth hurt, and cuz o' that we want her to have it. But…" She glanced at Evelyn, then back at me. "Girl's got no money."

"Ooo – kay." I swallowed hard and glanced at Evelyn. She looked at me with a smile and one raised eyebrow.

"She's got quite a business plan worked out. One of the professors over University helped her put together the dollars part. We gotta find some way help her. For her. And for Clarissa."

Evelyn's expression had not changed, but when I felt her foot under the table, stroking my leg, I sat back with my arms across my chest.

"How much are we talking here?"

"About eight thou."

"And that's for…?"

"Some new machines for the laundry and a special kind'a tank they say she needs for the car wash. Gotta have it for the septic permit. Town crew'll do the digging but she needs to buy the tank and pay the plumber."

"One of the professors looked at her plan?"

"Not just him. We got the state plumbing guys to spec out that septic stuff."

"C'mon Judith." Maybe she didn't think I was listening, but… "That's the third time just now you've said 'we'."

"Yeah." She looked around the room like she was concerned somebody was listening in, but if they were it was not obvious. "There's me and a few others on the board."

"Alright, tell me…" I was thinking of the rules, how stuff is supposed to happen, and where it goes if things aren't done right. "How's that game gonna fly?"

"Arnie, I know what y'er thinking. If we can, we'll let her announce it at the Public Meeting, let it be known she's got the money in place, try to discourage somebody else from thinkin' 'bout outbidding her." She shrugged. "She's got her big girl pants on, knows it c'n still happen."

When I glanced again at Evelyn, our eyes locked. I saw her head nod, just the tiniest bit, and the way the corners of her mouth lifted.

I turned back to Judith. "If you can pull this off," I said, "We'll spot her that money. One condition."

Judith looked at me with a question mark in her face but didn't ask the obvious.

"Far as anybody knows…" I looked around the room. All eyes were on the band, which appeared to be almost ready to go on break. "Doris Carson somehow landed herself a bank loan. We have nothing to do with what she's got going."

On the way home, I pointed out that if Blondie had actually gotten a loan from a bank they'd likely see her as a big risk and set her interest rate high. "What I know of *her*," I said, "there's very little risk in this deal. Our money'll be safe with Doris Carson." Evelyn didn't reply, just reached over and squeezed my hand.

* * * * *

For me, it all came together during that Thursday evening's rehearsal when a secret meeting was held in the cluttered shack out on the wharf. Jernegan and Fisher were both there, so was Diamond Lil, myself, and the other two rich bankers; Silverspoon and Golder. This was the point when The Reverend would prove to the skeptics how rich they'd become, if only they'd fork over their cash for shares in the Electrolytic Marine Salts Company. He'd warned us,

Look down across the beach
Far as your eyes can reach
For nary, nary a word
Should be overheard.

While we cluster close by like a gaggle of schoolgirls, Fisher hauls up the accumulator, sticks in his hand, and comes up with a chunk of gold. We are astounded to see what he's got, and so the haggling begins.

JERNEGAN   Just a buck a share;
                                  That certainly is fair

KINNEY   Sounds fair enough to me.

SILVERSPOON   Make mine twenty;
                                  That seems plenty.

DIAMOND LIL   Make mine thirty;
                                  Deal's not dirty.

GOLDER   I'll take fifty;
                                  That sounds nifty.

JERNEGAN   Bid a bit bigger, come on along!
                                  Make it one hundred, you can't go wrong!

KINNEY   I'll break the record, and I'll take the flush,
                                  But you better be sure it's all hush, hush.

JERNEGAN   All goes well, all goes fine.
                   Just sign your names on the dotted line.
                   And lose no time to write up your checks
                   And we'll all be in gold up to our necks!

KINNEY   Gold, gold from the salt sea waters;
                   Plenty of gold for our sons and daughters.

We dance about the stage, giddy at what we've done and our wonderfully good fortune. Of course I as Arnie, having read the script knew that Fisher was a diver and had salted that worthless contraption but I, as Kinney, believed what I was told and fell for it. Hook, line, and checkbook.

I wasn't the only one waiting for the big day, to stand before the town and tell a story that most knew but would still find hilarious. How could those rubes back then have been so easily deceived?

Laundromat

I had never seen such a large crowd in Flagg's Point. Special Town Meetings rarely draw such numbers but this time there must have been close to three hundred. The fire hall was jammed full and they had to remove all of the trucks and ambulances to accommodate late arrivals. An early-winter snow had mostly melted but there were slushy remnants underfoot – the crowd tracked crunchy sand into the hall but nobody seemed to care.

Checking off the voters held up the line, forcing Chester to delay opening until a full fifteen minutes past the scheduled start. As usual, Buster sat on the left, towards the rear, surrounded by his posse. Jake and Marlene sat quietly on the right, patiently waiting for the debates to begin.

Chester thumped the microphone and looked around at the crowd. Judith sat at the table behind him along with the other board members, and Marilyn St. Claire sat off to the side but still out front. Evelyn and I were in the front row, but as the committee had been dissolved there would be little call for me to speak.

Electing the moderator, and then waiting for him to read his usual instructions, took the first ten minutes. There was only one article on the warrant, and he read it off. Written in the arcane language of the town meeting warrant, it asked if the town would approve expending the money to purchase the building and make certain repairs and upgrades.

"What will you do with this?" he asked.

Jake was the first one up. "I move we accept it as written," he called out in a clear voice. Judith chimed in with the second.

When the moderator asked if there was any discussion, Buster was on his feet. "Yes, Mr. Loman," the moderator rumbled.

"This is the same thing we already voted down," he said, jutting out his jaw. "Why are we bringing it up ag'in?"

The moderator turned to Chester, who had already risen. "Mr. Taylor?"

"Buster," he began. "This is not the same proposal. This is from a committee of your neighbors, and you were specifically invited to be a part of it."

"So what has changed?"

Marilyn rose and was recognized. "We have identified new uses, included an estimate for the roof, tightened up the cost projections, and even have someone lined up that's planning to bid on leasing the laundry and car wash." When she looked around at the size of the crowd I was sure I saw a smirk.

"Someone wants to lease the laundry?" Buster looked around the room, craning his neck and looking stupefied. "Can you say who that is?"

"C'mon, Buster," chided Chester. "You know how that works. We ask for sealed bids, then we open them all during a selectman's meeting where everybody can watch."

A small commotion was heard from the right side, near the middle. When I glanced over, I spotted Blondie standing.

"Miss Carson," the moderator called out. "You have the floor."

"I am that person." Blondie spoke in a loud, clear voice, lifting one finger in affirmation. "I want to start that business so I can have something better for my daughter Clarissa. I have put together a business plan, and have the money lined up." She looked around the room. "I know what the rules are. I hope the winning bid is mine. After that I hope you all stop by wash your cars and trucks, use my laundry machines." Then she sat down, to a sprinkling of applause.

Buster shot her a furious glance. I couldn't help but hear him ask one of his friends, "where'd *she* dig up that money?" His neighbor shrugged but didn't appear to reply.

"Are there more comments?" The moderator looked around the room. "Do you want me to read the article again?" A loud chorus confirmed the crowd, having heard it once, didn't want to hear it again.

"We will now vote," he announced. "As before, this will be a written ballot."

People sat in their seats, waiting for the line to get short before rising. An enthusiastic crowd clustered around Blondie – most appeared to be her age. At one point I saw Jake go over to speak with her but Buster seemed to be avoiding that side of the room. I did find it puzzling that Susan Loman was seated next to Bethany Williams, near the front on the right and several rows from Buster.

The atmosphere crackled with expectation as resident after resident stepped up and dropped their ballot into the big wooden box with the padlock. Evelyn and I stood in line to take our turn, then returned to our seats to sweat out the verdict.

Judith wandered over to where we sat. "Whaddaya think, Arnie?"

"Crowd seems a bit bigger this time."

"Two hundred eighty four," she replied. "Better'n double last time."

"Gotta mean something."

"Last time it was all Buster's friends came out, shot it down. Hundred 'leven of 'em."

"Looks to me…" Evelyn glanced about the crowded room. "Like Blondie's got a few friends here too."

"Doris Carson's got herself some friends," said Judith, laughing softly. "And her friends got friends."

The moderator stepped to the microphone and spoke up. "Any here hasn't voted yet but wants to?" When nobody else came forward, he nodded to the clerk. The room fell silent while two hundred and eighty-four slips of paper were sorted, tabulated, counted, and re-counted. Two hundred and eighty-four people held their breath when the clerk handed a slip of paper to the moderator.

He looked it over carefully and turned back to the microphone. "One hundred-ten nays," he intoned. "And one hundred-seventy four…" His voice was drowned out by a huge cheer from the center-right of the room. I turned to look and saw Blondie being hugged by a mob of thirty people all at once with a noisy crowd clamoring for their turn. Susan and Bethany were in that crowd. I spotted Buster heading out the door, alone.

The insistent pounding of the gavel quieted the room just long enough to hear the moderator call out "do I hear a motion we adjourn?" I'm not sure he ever got that motion.

Surging and shoving, the crowd flowed out into the parking lot. "See what you did?" laughed Evelyn.

"Me?" I do confess I was pleased by the outcome, but hardly felt responsible for it. I spotted Judith elbowing her way over. "Arnie… Evelyn. Wait up."

"See how it works?" she asked, huffing and puffing from working her way through the jubilant crowd.

"I see how it turned out," I replied.

"She done told her friends her bank loan depended on passing this thing."

"When's the bid going out?"

"Tomorrow's the paper's deadline, we'll have it in, keep it open three weeks. That's as tight as we can get it and stay legit."

"So for her, it's now a waiting game."

"That's the deal," Judith replied, preparing to head down the street. She turned back momentarily in our direction. "If I were you," she added, keeping her voice just above a whisper, "I wouldn't go putting my checkbook away just yet."

"Any chance," Evelyn asked me, "this vote can be turned over?"

"What the rules say," I replied, "takes a bigger number of voters, and only after a petition forces another meeting."

"So they'd need – say – three hundred to show up?"

"Yeah," I said. "And then a majority of that if they'll reverse tonight's outcome."

* * * * *

The final curtain went down and we stepped to the front to take our bows. By this point Jernegan and Fisher had already decamped with the proceeds of the stock issue, leaving unpaid bills and fleeced investors wondering what had happened. Me, Kinney? The Gold Digger took me on, even though my fortune had vanished, having been rowed across the bay to Eastport with the two scoundrels. Guess I, or at least Mr. Kinney, got what was coming.

Many times during the performance the audience responded, sometimes with applause and other times with groans. I think some were delighted to see the pompous Kinney relieved of his wealth and fall into the clutches of Diamond Lil and I tried to push that point. "This play is already over the top," Parker had told us all before starting dress rehearsals, "if you can take it down that road even farther, go for it."

It became clear how many had seen the earlier performance, ten years back and before Evelyn and I arrived in Flagg's Point, because they were the ones who knew what was coming. They apparently enjoyed the re-telling, but when Tiffany stepped forward for her bow, the crowd leapt to its feet. Pauli'Nee's closing song still echoed in my head, and I heard a number of kids trying to sing it on their way out of the door.

> *To heck with the gold, there's herring in the bay.*
> *Ory, get your dory, and we'll catch them every day.*
> *Big fish, little fish, get 'em while you can*
> *Roll 'em up in corn meal, and fry 'em in a pan.*
>
> *To heck with the gold, there's herring in the bay.*
> *Lubec, America's where you want to stay.*
> *Seven million fishes with a silver hue*
> *Jump from the water in the foggy dew.*
>
> *To heck with the gold, there's herring in the bay.*
> *Hey nonnie, nonnie, and a hey, hey, hey!*

"Why'd you guys pick just now to tell this story again?" Judith asked me the next day. I'd stopped by at Annie's Place and she followed me through the door.

"Don't look at me," I protested. "Go ask Harry Parker that question."

"I did," she scoffed. "He really din't say nothing."

"You think there was some kind of hidden agenda?"

She gave me that look that said that, once again, I didn't get it. "Suggesting to the town that following hollow promises leads nowhere?" Continuing to stare at me, it was like she thought I was holding something back. "I'm quite sure that's got nothing to do with our new guy down Washington. Or our illustrious governor."

"Judith," I shrugged. "What're you trying to say?"

She stared at me with pursed lips. Maybe now it was her that was holding back. Or maybe she was right – it *was* me. "Guys!" she grumped, turning to leave. "One lies and the other friggin' swears to it."

Blondie's Suds

It was a gorgeous June evening and time for a beer. Today it had broken eighty, but only for a short spell. The scent of seaweed wafted in from the porch and the birds called to each other and the town had come back to life, just like it always does. The day had been the sort we had all been dreaming of, all winter long: too long in coming, and too soon past.

I had no idea Lisa was back in town, but there she was, casually lounging in Annie's Place, enjoying her glass of wine. "It must be spring," I said, sliding into the seat next to her. "The flowers are out and Lisa from Pennsylvania has returned!"

"See some things happening," she said as I dropped down next to her.

"Good things I hope."

"Likely so." She took a sip of wine and sat back eyeing me, one eyebrow hitched high.

I gestured to Annie for a beer. "We can start with Keisha."

"The black girl who beats everyone on the pool table?"

"That she does." I chuckled recalling how she had manhandled me on that table. "Moved back to town, landed a scholarship at the University. Plans to take up counselling."

"That's cool. So she's given up waiting on tables?"

"Prob'ly not yet, but soon enough. Even put a down payment on a place up on the North Road."

"I see something's happened at that old building coming into town."

"You like?"

"You're asking me?" She laughed. "I like what I see. But nobody's asking me to pay for it." The big town vote was scarcely talked about any more, having taken place seven months and a dreary winter earlier.

"Some of it," I replied, hoisting my beer, "is paying for itself."

"You mean like 'Blondie's Suds'?"

"You remember her, right?" Lisa gave me a quizzical look. "Doris Carson?"

"Already washed my car there. That made me happy. And it's good to see the laundry is up and running. That's something people need. Specially visitors."

"You should'a seen it back in March. Every car and pickup in town was lined up. Sheriff told her she was blocking the highway, had to give people a number, have 'em come back."

"That was when she opened?"

"Actually, she busted her butt, got it running two days before the blizzard clobbered us. She figured everybody'd want to get cleaned up after the snow melted. I never saw so many shiny cars and trucks 'round here." I drained my beer and signaled to Annie for a refill. "Heard she nearly ran out of soap."

"How about the rest of the place?"

"I'm sure you saw the new roof. That part we had to pay for. We got together a work party to clean up the lot and get some of the painting done. Even talked me into putting the gloves on." I chuckled recalling that day, everybody from the kids to us old farts, all pulling together and everybody seeing the improvement in the town as their paycheck. The lunch donated by the local eateries didn't hurt, either. Everybody liked the way they competed for 'Best Pizza' accolades.

"I remember there was talk of grant money." Lisa pulled a pen out of her purse and started idly doodling on a paper placemat. "Any of that come through?"

"We got two, not big but still helpful. Most of those funds've dried up with our new president." I had to laugh, thinking of how it all came down. "It was like the president and our governor teamed up to kill the town. Guess we fooled 'em."

"So you paid for this yourselves, at least mostly."

"For the most part." I raised my glass in honor of the town's effort. "Together, we made it happen."

Maybe I was so preoccupied talking with Lisa, who hadn't been in town since the previous August, that I didn't notice Buster had taken up his new-found position behind the bar. Annie had already returned to the kitchen and was busily preparing a clinking tray of glassware for the dishwasher but Lisa had her head down, concentrating on her doodle.

"Whatsamatter," he laughed, looking at Lisa. "Not cold 'nuff for ye down Pennsylvania way?"

"Since when…" I spotted the glint in her eye as she turned towards him, and the way the laugh-lines next to her eyes lifted. "Have you worked *that* side of the bar?"

"Got a problem with it?"

"Not at all." She took the last sip of wine and passed the empty glass across to him, glancing up momentarily at his New

England Patriots cap. Jake came through the door and sat down on her other side. "Actually," she continued, "I am highly impressed."

"Hear that, Jake?" Buster drawled. "Lady sez she's 'highly impressed'."

"Yeah?" Jake waited for Buster to draw him a beer. He took the first swig and wiped his mouth on his sleeve. "You really think she's the *only* one?"

The evening's band arrived and started humping gear across the threshold. I didn't know this group, a three-piece combo including a kid that looked to be maybe twelve, a middle-aged woman, and a man that had to be eighty sporting a long silvery pony-tail and a jaunty black Derby. Annie knew how to pick 'em, so I called Evelyn on my cell to see if she could come down and join us.

When Lisa spread her doodle out on the bar and lifted it up for all to see, I did a double-take. She'd sketched out a lovely sign, complete with a unique logo for Blondie's Suds. "Hey," I said, "that's something!"

"It's kind'a what I do," she replied with a shrug. "Think she'd like it?"

"I'm sure she would." Jake spun around to look it over, nodding appreciatively, and Annie came out of the kitchen.

"That's jist what that girl needs," said Buster, attracted by the others.

"If she wants it," Lisa said, "I can draw it up bigger so a shop can make it. Got my stuff back at the cottage." She paused for a second and looked up. "I did see something else on my way in." I wasn't sure if she was addressing Jake or me, but when he didn't reply I did.

"Pretty great view, ain't it."

"Spectacular," she marveled. "Never saw that before."

"Hah!" Jake guffawed. "Lived here all my life. I never seen it before, neither."

"Used to be the ruins of a fish packing plant down there, stopped operating years ago. Had some nasty stuff needed to be cleaned up," I told her. "Now it's more than just a great view and new digs for the Historical Society. That bunch worked long hours getting it looking like that."

"But that's only part of it," Jake added. "It's also good for our shellfishing guys. They always been after them flats, just couldn't get down there. Now they got a place to park their trucks and walk down."

Lisa looked at me with a bit of a frown. "Arnie," she said, "sounds like there's something you guy's aren't saying."

Perhaps she was more perceptive than I knew, maybe it was something in my voice. I turned toward the bar and signaled Buster for a refill. "That job got done just under the wire. The contractors beat the weather, but if they hadn't..." The way she looked at me I knew she was not about to let it drop. "The lion's share of the cost was paid by a Federal grant from the EPA. Just when they got it wrapped up, that well suddenly went dry. Those 'Brownfield Grants' are now history, killed two more projects in Flagg's Point alone."

"I assume," she said, quiet-like, "you're still talking about our illustrious president."

"That's not all that guy's tried to do to us," interjected Jake. "Our Coast Guard. They almost got cut off at the knee too." I knew he'd taken the loss of the *Mary Lynne* with her three men hard and thought the coasties had done more than anyone could ask. If they lost what little they had to work with, who'd be next?

"And," Jake continued, "How 'bout that coal-junk they're looking to put back in our air now? All the fly-ash and other stuff gonna come down where we fish. He never ast what *we* might think o' that. The money his buddies're gonna make from *that* comes out'a our hide."

"Wish I c'ud say I didn't vote for him," Buster grumbled. "He does things s'posed ta help them what voted *for* him, does things *to* ever body else. At least..." He lifted an armload of empty glassware and turned toward the kitchen, "he says we're still getting' us a friggin wall down Texas."

Conversation ceased for a moment while we watched the band getting ready. Turned out the kid played an electric twelve-string and the old dude was a fiddler. The woman? Maybe she could've been the kid's mother, but she was also the drummer. The fiddler pulled a note, and the kid tuned to it.

Jake leaned along the bar, towards me. "That old guy there," he said, pointing across the floor. "He writes some crazy lyrics. Annie swears he's amazing on that thing." Lisa turned back to me while they completed their set-up.

"So tell me," she asked. "How'd things work out for Tiffany?"

"Girl's going places. Moved up to the high school and made honor roll. Plays small forward on the varsity team. Hear there's college scouts coming 'round, giving her a second glance and pestering the coaches."

Buster stood before us, his bulk blocking the view beyond. "You better not let that kid get ahold 'a the damn ball." He put his hands on his hips and leaned back, stopping all talk with his rollicking laughter. "Tiffy get's 'er mitts on it, you ain't *never* gettin' it back."

Just about the time the band started up, Evelyn came in. She welcomed Lisa back to town while I got her a glass of wine, then we went off to a nearby table to check out Annie's latest find.

Turned out the drummer was also a pretty mean singer and the kid played a strong lead guitar while chiming in on the vocals. As far as the fiddler, it was clear he'd rosin'd up that bow a few times and knew how to pull it. They launched into their first piece with the guitarist firing off some wild riffs and the drummer laying into the beat...

Grab your hat and take yer choice,
What's it gonna be, Roscoe?
Which way you a fixin' to go?
Some times you just gotta lay them cards down.

Fin